BOOKS BY SAME AUTHOR

2018: *Contemporary Issues in Taxation.* Author House Publisher, UK. ISBN 978154629109.

2012: *Financial Accounting for Executives, MBA.*Author House Publisher, UK. ISBN 978148178010.

2011: *International Finance for Developing Countries.* Author House Publisher, UK. ISBN 9781456781705.

2010: *Corporate Finance.* Author House Publisher, UK. ISBN 9781456781705.

2008: *Financial Management Skills for Non- Finance Managers.* Learn and Share Publishers. ISBN 9987425127.

APPLIED MANAGEMENT:
CHIEF EXECUTIVE OFFICERS
(CEOS) AND MANAGERS
HANDBOOK

LUCKY YONA

authorHOUSE

AuthorHouse™ UK
1663 Liberty Drive
Bloomington, IN 47403 USA
www.authorhouse.co.uk
Phone: UK TFN: 0800 0148641 (Toll Free inside the UK)
*   UK Local: 02036 956322 (+44 20 3695 6322 from outside the UK)*

Published by AuthorHouse 07/24/2020

ISBN: 978-1-7283-5477-4 (sc)
ISBN: 978-1-7283-5476-7 (e)

CONTENTS

ABOUT THE AUTHOR

Prof Dr.Dr.Lucky Yona lectures at Eastern and Southern African Management Institute (ESAMI) in Arusha, Tanzania. He holds a PhD in Finance from Euraka Univeristy in Switzerland, a Doctorate of Business Administration (D.B.A.), a Master's Degree in Business Administration (M.B.A.) as well as a Master's of Philosophy (M.Phil.) from Maastricht. Prof Yona's undergraduate accomplishments include a Bachelor's Degree in Commerce and a Bachelor's Degree of Theology. He is a Certified Public Accountant (C.P.A) and an experienced consultant and international trainer. Lucky has published several finance and accounting books and numerous articles in internationally known, peer-reviewed journals.

Prior to joining ESAMI Lucky worked with a variety of reputable institutions and companies at the senior level. Some of these positions included serving as Financial Administrator for African Medical and Research Foundation (AMREF), Business Manager for International School of Moshi (now United World Colleges, East Africa), College Bursar for Kilimanjaro Christian Medical College and Chief Accountant at Iscor Mining. In addition to these distinguished positions, Dr. Yona taught Financial Accounting and Taxation at Nyegezi Social Training Institute (now St. Augustine University in Tanzania). He is also involved in teaching various MBA courses at Eastern and Southern African Management Institute (ESAMI) Business School—a prestigious institution serving ten African countries.

FOREWORD

Effective governance and management require, among other capabilities, personal integrity as well as well as competence. Some people, when they hear the concept of 'good governance' mentioned, the first thing that comes to their mind is integrity and ethical leadership. Whereas these two traits are extremely important, sometimes managers fail to perform well because they lack a number of essential competencies, notwithstanding their high level of integrity.

The 'Applied Management: Chief Executive Officers and Managers Handbook' discusses a set of competencies required by Senior Managers, in particular Chief Executives. What I find most fascinating and instructive are (a) how to work well with the Board Members, (b) how to engage successfully with donors and other external stakeholders, (c) effective management of organizational assets, (d) proper management of financial resources and budget and (e) coping with challenges and risks arising from external environment, as well as from within the organization. The author successfully simplifies what are normally complex concepts and analytical methods and techniques. He provides many examples and illustrations, as well as self-testing exercises.

The book is particularly useful for those chief executives and managers who have limited formal training in financial management and related subjects.

Graduate students without formal training in finance will benefit from reading the book as it provides a simplified discussion on important topics, including (a) management of current assets (cash, debtors and stock or inventory), (b) preparation of financial budget, (c) financial reporting and understanding of financial statement, and (d) the basics of auditing.

I strongly recommend the book.

Prof Venantio Mvano, PhD
Eastern and Southern African Management Institute

ACKNOWLEDMGENT

There are many friends and collegues who have encouraged me to finish this manuscript, I highly appreciate the support accorded by all of you to help me complete this book. The support from my best friends, academic professional and practionioers in the area of management has contributed a lot on writing the book. I also appreciate my former current and previous employers who gave me the opportunity to save in management positions, from there I drew the experience which I thought it is important to document so that new generations desiring may tape the experiences.

The support given to me by Karah Garmoth by accepting to edit the whole book in a shoter time gave me the streght to finish the book. You have challenged me with your editing skills as you were trying to think in the same way I wanted the book to be.

I have dedicated this book to my only late daughter, Faith Lucky . Her life style, vision was geared towards leadership and management. I wish she should have lived to accomplish her vision and practice management and benefit from the experiences and knowledge documented .

Prof Dr.Dr. Lucky Yona
Phd (Finance), DBA (Banking), MBA (Finance), Mphil, CPA (T), Bcom (Accounting) B.Th

DEDICATION

This book is dedicated to my only,
late Daughter, Faith Lucky

PREFACE

This book is designed specifically for Chief Executive Officers (CEOs) and managers who are responsible for different management functions in their organizations. Chief Executive Officers and managers require a range of skills and knowledge to be able to function effectively in their positions. These positions must know and understand many management techniques and facets in order to make constructive day-to-day decisions and improve the performance of their organizations.

There is a commonly found knowledge gap for managers which has not yet been addressed in a single training or resource. Managers need knowledge not only in management of companies' financial and tangible assets but also in managing risks, managing crises, political challenges and many other issues. The majority of managers do not aquire these skills in their education training and these skills are not addressed in ongoing institution-run trainings either.

This book bridges the knowledge gap by addressing key management issues that may have a negative impact on organizations if they are not managed well but that may not be addressed in other educational or training sessions. This book will serve as a guide for managers so that they may learn and begin to utilize needed skills on how to approach some of the above listed challenges in their day to day operations.

Lucky Yona

CHAPTER 1

WORKING CONSTRUCTIVELY WITH YOUR BOARD OF DIRECTORS

1.1   Introduction

The first thing you need to know when taking on the role of CEO or Director of a new institution is who you are reporting to and how to relate to all board members of the organization that has appointed you. The Board of Directors is, in a sense, your employer as they represent the company shareholders and serves to safeguard shareholders' interests. As a company leader, you need to understand that it is the Board who confirms your employment, writes and provides you with a job description, decides on your remuneration, and evaluates your performance. And, in the end, it is the same Board that can choose to renew or not renew your contract. Considering all of this, it should become clear to you that the relationship between you, the chair of the Board and all Board members matters a lot. In fact this relationship may determine whether you can continue working with the organization.

This chapter will give you a general understanding of the role of Board of Directors, tips on how to relate with the Board chair and members, the importance of Board committees, better skills for connecting with and reporting to the Board as well as different dynamics you may face in creating and maintaining your relationship with the Board. Understanding these issues will help you work more effectively for the organization and will also help you gain favor in your professional role.

1.2. Board of Directors' Responsibilities

When looking at the responsibilities of the Board of Directors, we must start with clarifying that the Board of Directors does not have the mandate to run the organization's day to day activities. The Board holds different key responsibilities that focus on ensuring proper corporate governance systems and supporting solid accountability and peak performance of the entire organization. If the Board fails to perform these responsibilities correctly, loop-holes may be created that allow company CEOs and managers to underperform their duties.

One of the most significant responsibilities of the Board of Directors is to create and drive the strategic direction of the organization. This is achieved by forming the vision and mission statement of the organization. The Board of Directors also has the sole responsibility of approving company policies that support these vision and mission statements. In order for these to be created in a useful way, CEOs and management teams should formulate company policies and present them to the Board for approval. Once the company policies have been approved by the Board of Directors, the management has the responsibility to implement them.

In addition to the responsibilities mentioned above, the Board of Directors also appoints the Chief Executive Officer and has the role of identifying key areas of risk in the organization and establishing policies to prevent and mitigate risk. A final yet equally important role of the Board is to create company performance indicators.

1.3. Your Relationship with the Board

As the company CEO or manager, a positive relationship with the Board of Directors is vital. However, to create this positive relationship, you need to understand the dynamics of relating to the Board of Directors. At times some Board members would like to intervene and micromanage the organization but this is outside of their role and responsibility. All parties should understand that the responsibility of organizational management lies in the hands of its CEO and management team-- not with the Board of Directors. Once you understand this, clarifying your role and maintaining a supportive relationship between you, your management team and the Board of Directors becomes much easier.

Most of the time, the Board will provide guidance and deliberate company policy issues within Board meetings rather than through dialogue with individual Board members. Therefore as a CEO or manager, you should ensure that you organize and present all issues requiring Board discussion and decision-making are added to the Board meeting agenda. In your role, you cannot underestimate how important maintaining this relationship is but a poor relationship between the CEO, management, and/or Board of Directors may undermine business performance. Poor relationships lead to unresolved conflicts between Board members and the CEO and may delay critical, strategic decision-making.

There are several techniques which Chief Executive Officers can use to establish a healthy and productive relationship with Board members. One of the most effective ways of maintaining a strong relationship is to regularly seek counsel and advice from the Board on all issues within their mandate as Board members. When you do this, you prevent future resentment from Board members when something does not go as planned. Informal relationships with Board members outside of the formal Board meetings are also crucial for building stable relationships with Board members. It is through these informal meetings that you can begin to understand who the Board members are and can use this knowledge initiate open, professional conversations.

Remember that each Board member was included in the Board of Directors because of personal or professional qualities he or she demonstrated. Keep an open mind when listening to different opinions from Board members as their ideas will complement your own knowledge and help you to lead your company more productively. The diversity of ideas from the Board will enhance your understanding as each member's opinions develop from their unique skills and expertise.

1.4. Meeting with the Chairman of the Board

The Board chairperson bears the final responsibility for all Board decisions. As a company CEO or manager, he or she is only person whom you are required to report to directly on your day-to-day organizational affairs. It would be a disaster if you attempted to interact with all Board members about daily organizational activities and would create confusion amongst the team and so you must ultimately understand that the Chairperson of the Board is your one and only boss.

While the Board chair does need to know about the daily organizational activities, daily meetings with the Board chair are not healthy. Scheduling weekly or monthly meetings between you as the CEO or manager and the Board chair is more appropriate as this will keep the chair informed about daily activities without major infringement on your time.

Just as daily meetings are not healthy, as a company CEO or manager, you also cannot wait to interact with the Board chair only during structured, quarterly Board meetings as this practice may hamper your productivity and impair better business performance. Having formalized weekly or monthly meetings are vital for you as a CEO or manager to keep the Board informed on organizational happenings and to be assured that what you are doing in your role has the blessing of the Board. The Board chair will interact with other Board members when essential issues arise that require the whole Board's support and the chair will help you gain their consent. With modern technology, distance should not be a barrier to regular meetings since meetings can be held via video conferences which save cost and travel time and support flexible scheduling for all involved.

1.5 Working with Board Committees

Usually issues and discussion are held through Board committees before final deliberations are held in formal Board Meetings. While the number of Board committees and committee members will vary from one company to another, their purpose is primarily the same; Board committees are formed by the Board itself to handle complex organizational issues that cannot be managed by the entire Board. Committees also make policy recommendations utilizing the skills and expertise of specific Board members for approval by the whole Board. Through committees, more input is received from individual Board members and so decision-making quality is enhanced.

As a company CEO or manager, your role is to provide information and support to the Board committees so that they can make policy recommendations to the Board. Board committees may include: Auditing, Finance, Board Development, Standing, and Fundraising committees. Each of these board committees has different functions to perform and may require a great deal of information from you as CEO or manager to support their tasks. It is important that you facilitate easy information and knowledge transfer between the organization's management team and these committees so that their committee meetings and input are beneficial to the organization as a whole.

1.6 Common Challenges CEOs and Managers Face in Working with the Board

Most CEOs and Managers face similar challenges in working with the Board of Directors. Below are some common challenges that company CEOs and Managers face while carrying out their responsibilities:

1. **Over-interference by the Board:** Chief Executive Officers and managers often feel overwhelmed by Board members' interference in daily management responsibilities. This problem tends to arise when the Board does not adequately orient Board members on their role and responsibilities;

2. **Infrequent Board Meetings:** As a result of inadequate funding for Board meetings, some companies reduce the number of Board meetings. With few Board meetings, the pace of important decision-making is slow and ineffective.

3. **Conflicts of Interest:** At times Board members may participate on a Board of Directors to Board pursue their personal interests. When a CEO or Manager is unwilling to accommodate these personal interests, the Board member may become uncooperative in Board meetings.

4. **Personality conflicts:** It is possible for the Chief Exceutive Officer to have personality conflicts with board members because of various reasons. Not all Board members will easily get along with every CEO and/or Manager— issues that arose before joining the organization or past misunderstandings could impact the new working relationship. When personality conflicts arise, this poses challenges to the work of the CEO or Manager.

5. **Lack of collaboration:** When CEOs or Managers don't understand the importance of consulation with the Board of Directors, they often fail to seek the Board's opinions when making key decisions for the organization. CEOs and Managers should not abandon Board collaboration and risk losing constructive and beneficial feedback.

1.7 Conclusion

The chapter is an eye opener to Chief Executives and managers on how they should deal with the board of directors. Understanding how to relate with the board is the key success factor to sustainable organizational performance. The chapter highlights the importance of CEO's and managers to appreciate the role and responbsibilities of the board and how to relate with it as they perform their responsibilities.

The chapter also provides a brief discussion on how the Ceo's and should relate with the board chair and other board members professionally. It highlights further the role of board commitees and how the Ceo should work with them as they perform their duties on the behalf of the whole board.

Lastly the chapter has highlihted a number of challenges which Chief Excutives face as they deal with their boards and suggested some ideas on how the chief excutives should do in order to address different challenges they face. The Challenges discussed in this chapter they are not all inclusive for all organizations. Each organization might have different challenges. The discussion in the chapter is just an indicative issuies of challenges which CEO's face in their day to day working environment.

Practice Questions

Question 1

What are the possible causes of conflicts between company Chief Ecxcutive officers/Managers ?

Question 2

Discuss the possible challenges of working with the board. Are there any possible options to address the challenges?

Question 3

Discuss how the board can ensure effectiveness of the board committees.

Question 4

Why do managers or Chief Executive Managers fail to meet the expectations of the board of directors?

CHAPTER 2

MANAGEMENT OF FIXED ASSETS

2.1   Introduction

All institutions and business organizations, whether they are private or public, possess some type(s) of fixed assets. Management of these fixed assets is vital for organizations to achieve their visions and missions. Effective management of fixed assets requires competent procurement, usage, recording, retention, and disposal of these assets.

Proper management of fixed assets is essential for organizations to minimize loss resulting from fraud, misappropriation of, or theft of assets. Adequate control of fixed assets ensures appropriate utilization of these assets to ensure their longevity and to reduce organizational costs.

By being prudent in managing fixed assets, organizations benefit immensely. Not only are operative costs reduced through regular mainenance and timely repair of assets, good asset management can also help ensure that assets are not bought unneccessarily. A sound fixed asset management plan reduces preventable damage and breakdown of assets and helps CEOs and Managers stay abreast of the organization's inventory. At th same time, proper assets management allows management to identify what to dispose of and what to keep which ensures that quality, durable assets are on hand at all times.

Professional fixed asset management aids organizations beyond the obvious financial benefits.Manager should ensure that the company has good asset management. Though this is not an easy task but it is possible.

By setting up a proper fixed assets management system and appropriate internal control system, you will help ensure that the Organization minimizes theft of organizational assets. This will subsequently help stabilize the Organization through reducing repetitive assets.

2.2   What Constitutes a Fixed Asset

There are three main attributes of fixed assets. The first attribute of a fixed asset is durability which means that the asset is capable of existing for an extended period of time, usually at least a year. The second identifying attribute of a fixed asset is that the asset is not readily convertible to cash. A true fixed asset can be converted to cash but the process may not be straightforward and may take some time. The last recognizable attribute of a fixed asset is value. Fixed assets are generally worth quite a considerable amount of money. Examples of fixed assets include motor vehicles, machinery, aircrafts, land, buildings, and high quality equipment, fixtures, and furniture.

2.3   Management's Role in Safeguarding Companies' Fixed Assets

In addition to numerous management roles regarding decision-making for the betterment of an organization, management also has the sole responsibility of safeguarding their organization's fixed assets. This responsibility for fixed assets management is paramount to running a successful and profitable organization.

Because this is such an important role, management should immediately put in place and consistently monitor proper fixed assets policies that provide guidance to the company as whole about how assets will be procured, used, retained and disposed. These policies must also include appropriate internal control systems that spell out exactly how fixed assets must be procured, recorded, and used by employees for proper fixed assets management to be achieved.

Secondly, management should also ensure that there is proper documentation of assets procurement, usage, and assets disposal. All documentation of all matters related to fixed assets procurement should follow company policy.

Management should also consider what procedures are needed in regards to use, maintenance, and disposal of fixed assets without increasing unnecessary costs to the Organization. Part of this process should include assigning appropriate authorization persons or teams in each area of asset management from procurement to maintenance, usage and disposal.

2.4 Challenges in Managing Fixed Assets

As with all responsbilities CEOs and Managers hold, fixed assets management is not easy and can be particularly challenging with large organizations that have many fixed assets. Several common challenges in fixed asset management can lead to financial losses. CEOs and Managers should specifically watch and plan for the below listed issues:

1. **Improper procedures for the disposal of assets**
2. **Inadequate financial account records:** this can include mistakes in accounts recording, missing dates of purchases, misplaced code number, incorrect or missing cost recording.
3. **Inconsistent maintenance of the assets**: such as a lack of care for, inconsistent service or repair of assets
4. **Lack of Clear or Effective Theft Avoidance Policies**
5. **Poor Control of an Organizational Assets**
6. **Improper Authorization Procedures for Storage and Record-keeping**
7. **Lack of Necessary Skills in Assets Management:** skills and training are needed in assets planning and storage, record- keeping, auditing, and evaluation/assessment.

2.5 Best Practices in Fixed Assets Management

Fixed Assets Management is nothing new for many organizations. Over time, both public institutions and private institutions have put systems and procedures in place to manage their assets. Some of the best practices in Fixed Assets Management include:

a. **Ensuring that a definite asset management policy is place:** Good asset management policies allow organizations to easily facilitate their procurement, usage, custodianship of, and disposal of fixed assets,

b. **Conducting frequent and thorough staff trainings:** To avoid misuse of company assets, staff who are involved in managing assets must undergo training to understand how to use the assets accordingly to prevent misuse of the assets. Assets management certification now days exist and engaging staff in courses towards certification is a worthy investment

c. **Regularly checking inventory and disposing of unneeded fixed assets:**

For the Organization to retain appropriate assets, companies must conduct regular inventory/stock-taking to identify old, poor quality and unneeded assets so they may be disposed of. Regular stock-taking will help management stay aware of individual assets' state and existing lifespan.

Disposing of assets at the right time will help the organization receive some money back from the items,

d. **Reducing bureaucracy:** Unnecessary bureaucratic procedures create cumbersome procedures in procuring assets and disposing of assets and therefore reduce the efficiency of assets management.

e. **Introducing an assets tracking system:** Companies should invest in proper asset management software to help track their assets and keep good accounting through the use of a computerized fixed asset register.

f. **Developing and maintaining strategies for asset procurement and disposal:** Clear strategies should answer the questions of when, where, and how the company should aquire and dispose of assets. These strategies should be utilized whenever a decision about assets management is to be made.

g. **Verifying physical existance of items:** Item audits should be regularly scheduled to ensure the physical existence of items mimics the records.

h. **Enforcement of laws and regulations:** Companies must know and enforce rules and regulations set by the company itself, the government and other regulatory organizations to safeguard their assets. This goes hand in hand with establishing proper internal controls to achieve the objective of protecting company assets.

2.6. Corruption on procurement of Fixed Assets

One problematic area in assets management that requires special attention by management is reducing corruption and mitigating the negative effect of corruption in the procurement of fixed assets. If procurement is left without check, corruption in procurement is likely to occur and with negative impacts on the company or organization such as:

a. **Misuse of Organizational Assets:** For example, the authority-in-charge may decide to sell assets for their personal benefit or to use them as personal assets. Other workers will not have access to this privilege and therefore will feel discouraged and demoralized.

b. **Misuse of funds:** When corruption exists, items may be sold to benefit a few people and will then have to be replaced. This obviously wastes money that could be used to solve other needs of the Organization.

c. **Reduction in Creativity and Morality of Employees :** Faithfully employees are likely to be discouraged by corruption activities in the procurement if management does not fight corruption practices.

d. **Less accountability:** When no one is taking true responsibility for taking care of organizational assets, accountability throughout the organization decreases.

e. **Investors lose faith and pull out of the organization** – When fixed assets are funded by donorrs for example and corruption erupts in the process of procurement,it leads to over expenditure to the budget and can affect donors relationship to continue funding assets procurement.

2.7   Challenges in the procurement of Fixed Assets

The procurement of fixed assets for any organization involves huge investment of funds. If not done very carefully, a company may experience enormous financial loss and so prudent policies and procedures are important.

However, in the process of assets procurement, several challenges may arise, which may cause a company to incur unneccessary costs. If a company wishes to achieve value for money when procuring assets, attention must be paid to these challenges:

a. **Uncommitted/Unfaithful employees:** Assets procurement requires a specific skillset and extensive training. Therefore, companies should seek employees who are in it for the long-term and are committed to this field of business.

b. **Price Inflation:** Prices of assets are likely to change from time time due to inflation. Therefore, Keen budgeting and proper timing for procuring the assets can reduce costs.

c. **Unskilled/Inadequately trained employees:** In an effort to save funds, unskilled/inadequately trained employees may procure poor quality assets that are not durable and therefore need replaced frequently.

d. **Lack of thoughtful procurement planning :** Procurement of assets should not be hapazardly . Proper planning is impoerant to identify the need, determine the time, the how and the quantity of assets to meet

2.8   Conclusion

The chapter has outlined some of the potential challenges, areas of consideration, and best practices in the topic of fixed assets management.

Effective fiixed assets management involves the management of all procurement, maintenance and disposal procedures required throughout the life of an asset.

In all stages of fixed assets management, but particularly in the procurement stage, managers and CEOs must consider the legal framework existing in their own country and comply with the most up-to-date laws and regulations, especially if the institution is a public sector institution. Private companies face less restrictions to comply with the public procurements laws, regulations, and procedures except when they are collaborating or interfacing with a public sector institution.

As outlined above, management teams should always work to build the capacities of individual employees working in the the management of assets in their Organization as investment in capacity commitment to a career in assets management are more committed and educated in best practices and therefore management should encourage and support team members to pursue professional courses and certification.

Practice Questions

Question 1

What constitute fixed assets of an organization or company?

Question 2

Discuss potential challenges in managing fixed assets in the context ofpublic sector institutions.

Question 3

What needs to be done by organizations Chief Executive Officers or Managers to to improve asset management?

Question 4

What are likely key benefits of proper asset management in your organization or company?

Question 5

How does corruption affect asset management in your country? How can you mitigate these negative impacts?

Question 6

What are potential challenges in implementing asset tracking software in your organization or company?

CHAPTER 3

MANAGEMENT OF DONOR-FUNDED PROJECTS

3.1 Introduction

This chapter intends expand readers' knowledge and understanding of management of donor-funded projects and will be essential for managers of non-profit organizations or those working with non-profit organizations whereby the significant sources of funds are from donors. Donors being among the major stakeholders in these types of organizations, managers must recognize their need for technical and financial reports to assess the organizations's ability to implement project requirements as outlined in the partnership agreement. Donors use these reports for making decisions on whether to support or continue to support a project.

3.2 Characteristics of Donor-funded projects

Basic characteristics of Donor-funded projects are listed below and should be well understood by managers and CEOs working for or with donor-funded projects.

1. **Funding is never guaranteed** as all funding depends on donor contributions. These contributions will only be given when the project performance follows the funding agreements. Any actions

or spending outside of what is outlined in the funding agreement jeopardizes continued or future funding.

2. **Donor funded projects do have a lifetime** and therefore funds to implement the projects must be used within the allotted time. Without careful consideration of funding agreement timelines, projects may not be completed as expected.

3. **The Funding of donor-funded projects might be volatile or inconsistent.** There are times when donors change their priorities in funding and discontinue funding to your projects. When this happens, projects may risk ending before completion of objectives.

4. **All donor-funded projects require timely technical and financial reporting**. Delays in providing these reports may slow the release of funds or create donor disappointment.

5. **Stakeholders should be included in all stages of donor- funded projects.**

6. **All donor funding is backed by line-item budgets** that must be followed and submitted to donors in line with agreed- upon project activities.

3.3   Donor Funded Project Requirements

All donor-funded projects require the funding recipient to fulfill specific conditions given by the donor to maintain the donor/recipient relationship. These requirements often include assessment of project performance as well as technical and financial reporting. Adherence to donor requirements enhances the relationship and it creates the possibility of gaining additional funds by the same donors or other donors in the future. Therefore, managers need to pay careful attention to the details of all contractual agreements associated with the project. The credibility of an organization can quickly be eroded if managers ignore the needs of the project.

In the following sections, we will discuss in brief what project performance assessments and technical and financial reporting entails.

3.4 Project Performance Assessment

The performance of donor-funded projects is measured by established performance indicators, which vary from donor to donor. Even though each donor's key indicators for measuring project performance may differ, some of key performance indicators commonly used in donor-funded projects include:

a. **Quantitative data that shows direct results of project activities** such as the number of children immunized, the number of teachers trained, kilometers of roads constructed, etc.
b. **Output results assessed against the targets**
c. **Outcomes and impacts of the project**
d. **Cost-effectiveness** as determined through assessment of costs against budgets or costs against output

3.5 Budgeting for Donor-funded Projects

Budgeting is the quantitative plan of organizational expenses to be used during a specific period of time. Non-profit organizations should not overlook the process of budgeting because neglecting budgeting procedures may result in the organization omitting important programs or activities from their budgets. When activities are not included in the budget, it is unlikely that these activities will be funded by donors and so project implementation may be difficult or impossible. Budgets for donor-funded projects, must be clear and comprehensive.

Managers working for or with non-profit organizations must also beware of the risk of under-budgeting as the donor/recipient relationship may be damaged if more funding is sought before all promised activities have been completed.

Under normal circumstances, when managers write a winning proposal to donors, objectives and programs which they intend to implement during the project lifetime are clearly defined and explained.

However, it often happens that managers, especially when writing budgets themselves, do not match all the project activities with the correct financial cost. This is particularly likely to occur if the manager is not trained or is inexperienced in writing budgets. Therefore, it is advisable that managers or other relevant persons do the technical proposal writing and involve accountants or other financial personel in creating the proposal budget before submitting it to donors.

Another critical issue in preparing budgets for donor-funded project proposals is understanding donor funding preferences. Certain project activities are likely to be funded by the donors while others are not; knowing these preferences will save managers time and the frustration of requesting funds that will never be granted. It is essential, then, to obtain information about funders before embarking on proposal budget development. To clarify further, an example of expenses that might not be in favor of some donors is overhead costs. While most donors are likely to fund to a maximum of 3% to 12% of overhead expenses, some will not support any of the overhead costs. Donors are, in general, more interested in project costs (implementation of activities) than in overhead costs. For that reason, always include an item line for overhead costs when submitting a project proposal. Find out the donor's policy on overheads and adjust the proposal accordingly.

Budget formats in donor-funded projects have specific implications. While some donors are very strict in how the budget should be prepared and submitted, others have no defined format. For those donors who require a particular presentation, a template will be provided and when requesting funds, it is important to adhere to the required format so as not to have your request denied.

Budget submission dates for donor-funded projects are another critical issue which managers need to consider. Donors have dates set as deadlines for budget submissions and a delay in submission may delay the funder from releasing funds needed for implementing your project. Budgets should always be submitted on time and sent to the respective offices to avoid a delay in funds provision.

3.6   Fundraising

Fundraising is not an easy job and the job includes much more than just completing funding proposals. To effectively fundraise either locally or internationally it is crucial to consider the following steps:

1. **Identify possible funders.** There are different organizations that might be willing to fund your project. However, despite the fact that they can fund your project, you need to understand their interest . Funders have diferent interests and are not likely to fund any projects outside their interest.

2. **Submit letters of inquiry:** Some funding organizations will not require you to submit a complete funding proposal but request a letter of inquiry. The letter of inquiry is basically a concept paper or outline of your request after which the donor will request a formal proposal if interested.

3. **Submit the funding proposal:** Once you have received a a proposal request from the donor organzation, watch deadlines carefully and submit your proposal on time and in the correct format.

4. **Do not take rejection from a funder personally:** Even if you follow all the guidelines and have a worthy project, there will be instances when your organization does not get the grant it needs. Remember that the funding agency has numerous applications for a limited amount of money. The vast majority of submitted proposals fail, so do not be put off but rather learn from failure! You may want to write a brief letter or email to the funder asking the reasons for the rejection. The answer may suggest how to improve the proposal or even request an improved re-submission.

5. **Maintain a positive relationship with donor organzations:** Building a good, trusted relationship with your donor is very important. While cooperation may not feel natural since the funder may request long and complicated reports and may restrict funding until reports have been provided. Misunderstandings can lead to communication problems. Don't forget that donors are dependent on their supporters, who, in turn, need reassurance that their money is spent well and this reassurance is found through detailed and up- to-date reporting.

Some ways to improve donor relationships are:

- After receiving funds, write a letter of acknowledgment and thanks.
- Send regular reports as requested by the donor.
- Keep the costs as per agreement
- If two or more donors are supporting your project, then the area of support should be clearly defined and communicated to the donor.

3.7 Accounting for Donor-funded Projects

Financial accounting for donor funds is a must for every organization. Therefore it is essential that the organization ensures that proper books are kept. Whether manually or electronically prepared using accounting software, the accounting records will provide information needed on donor financial reports and will provide evidence for any required audits. Basic accounting requirements include maintaining proper cash books and a separate ledger for each donor-funded project. Separation helps avoid mixing transactions and ensures appropriate accountability of funds provided by different funders.

It is also necessary to keep a separate bank account for each donor-funded project to help with reconciling donor funds. Bank reconciliations statements should be prepared at the end of each month for each funding source.

Opening separate bank accounts

When your organization is funded by different donors, opening a bank account for each funding source is highly recommended and is often required by donors. Having separate bank accounts for each funder facilitates easy cash flow monitoring and simplifies fund reconciliation with donors. Managers and CEOs should carefully look through funding agreements because opening a bank account is a common clause included by donors.

3.8   Grant Reconciliation Reports

While managing donor funds, problems can arise when funds are not received on time or in full. Funding delays may be due to delay by donors releasing funds as agreed, international banking system problems, or transfer problems. At times, the money received by an organization may not be the same amount as the money released by the donor. Accountants need to prepare a grant reconciliation report to help the management to know and understand what funds were received and when so that the administration does not authorize expenditures beyond the available funds. Reconciliation reports can also help in making follow up on delays in the release of funds caused by donors.

3.9   Donor Financial Reports

Donors will also require financial reports to see whether the funds given were used for the intended purposes. Financial reports required by donors do not necessarily follow a specific format but should be in line with international accounting standards. Some donors have a particular format that they require as far as financial statements are concerned and so all accountants in your organization need to be aware of specific requirements of each donor. Documents from donors related to financial issues must be made available to your organization's accountants so that they understand exactly what the donor needs from them.

Consequences of late financial reports to donors

Delaying financial reports or not producing them at all will cause serious problems for the organization. The responsible manager must ensure that proper financial statements are provided and submitted on time and as agreed upon by the organization. The following are some of the consequences which may occur if financial reports are late or incomplete:

- **Delay in release of funds by donors**
- **Poor donor/recipient relationship:** Donors will begin to form a negative image of your organization.

- **Donor withdrawal:** In some cases, donors will terminate funding for the organization and so ongoing projects will suffer.
- **Delays in project implementation:** When one project is delayed or funding is withdrawn, current and future projects will be impacted
- **Reputation of your organization compromised:** Potential donors may have a negative image of your organization and become less inclined to provide support.

3.10   Financial problems related to Donor-funded projects

Donor-funded projects tend to experience some financial problems. While some of these problems can be resolved within the organization itself when it aligns itself to its mission and objectives, other issues originate from the donor and cannot be resolved internally. The following are some of the financial-related problems associated with donor-funded projects because of organizational and donor-related issues:

a) Lack of adequate funds to finance projects,
b) Challenges in identifying funding sources,
c) Conditions laid out by donors (i.e. all funding must be used in a particular country),
d) Incompetant finance staff to manage projects,
e) Lack of stakeholder involvement,
f) Bureaucratic procurement procedures,
g) Under-budgeting during the proposal stage,
h) Donor reluctancy in funding certain costs (i.e. donors do not want their funds to be used towards salary costs because they are a 'core' cost or will only fund salaries for persons directly involved in the funded project may be covered. Salary costs accrued for time spent developing projects, ensuring democratic, inclusive, and accountable working within the network, meeting legal obligations, reporting to donors, and running the office are often not covered,
i) Financial sustainability, NGOs and their stakeholders must develop resource mobilization strategies and start exploring creative alternatives to traditional sources of funding to create long-term sustainability,

j) Highly dependency on external donor-funds which leads to donor-driven projects. In some countries, donors have withdrawn funding while projects are in their middle years,

k) Overspending due to failure in budget management, poor cost estimating, and inadequate attention to tendering and contract creation.

3.11 Technical Reports

Apart from financial reporting, management has the responsibility of producing a technical report that outlines the implementation of activities conducted as stipulated in the donor contract. The technical report should give information on all technical aspects of the funded project such as compliance to health standards, construction specifications, and project successes and challenges.

The technical report depends so much on the nature of the project itself and cannot be a copy of any other project rather tailored one to meet all the specifications as per donor agreements

3.12 Auditing of Donor Funded Projects

All donors would like to ensure that the funds give are effectively used in accordance with the project agreement. Therefore, apart from the internal audit or the normal external audit as required by the organization board, donors may also require special audits to be done for their funded projects. In these cases, donors might direct their own staff to conduct the audit or may select an auditing firm to check the accounts of the specific project. The auditing can either be a continuous for ongoing projects or for one projects at a specific period especially for those projects that are coming to an end.

Auditins is particularly important to the because it allows them to know if their funding has been utilized for the intentend purpose so that they can make the right choices about whether to continue supporting a project or not. In cases where auditing findings reveal misconduct or misuse of funds, donors are likely to cease supporting the project.

3.13   Managerial problems related to donor-funded projects

The management of donor-funded projects is challenging and managerial problems may arise from the donor or from within the organization which impair the performance of the project. Delays in the completion of a project or poor project performance can occur when the following common managerial problems occur:

a) Lack of serious commitment from the recipient,
b) Lack of early capacity building to implement the project effectively,
c) Micromanagement of projects by donor because donor lacks trust in project leaders,
d) When project implementation period is too short and therefore not achievable,
e) Strict conditions imposed by donors which impair timely project intervention,
f) Poor negotiation terms by the government on donor-funded projects,
g) Short-term interests prioritized over long-term gain,
h) Lack of proper planning by management,
i) Lack of political goodwill in accepting donor conditions.

3.14   Conclusion

This chapter has, in a nutshell, discussed how to deal with donor-funded projects. The topic is ideal for all chief Executive officers and managers of non -profit organizations which depend on donor funds to finance their projects. The chapter has also highlighted processes organizations should use to seek funding from different donors and how to account funds and auditfunded projects. It also discussed briefly the managerial problems related to management of such projects. Company Chief Executive Officers and managers can benefit more if they understand the key issues discussed and apply them into their day to day activities as they perform their roles.

Practice Questions

Question 1

The Donor project cycle involves a number of stages. The stages involved include identification stage, preparation, appraisal, negotiations, funding agreement and signing, implementation and supervision, and ex-post evaluation. What are likely to be critical activities by donors and recipients in each of these stages?

Question 2

What measures are necessary in reducing financial and managerial problems related to donor-funded projects?

Question 3

A ministry is considering the establishment of an industrial estate on the outskirs of a main township. The proposed area is currently predominantly farmland. There are some funders interested in the project but funding has not yet been secured. The ministry has approached you to be one of the project team members and one of the terms of reference given to your team is to prepare the budget of the project for the next three years. Complete the following tasks using this information.

   a) Enumerate the project goals: Identify all possible project activities that are likely to take place during the implementation of the project.
   b) Prepare a budget based on the activities you have identified in part a.
   c) How will you advise the ministry to go about sourcing the funds for the budget you have prepared?
   d) What assumptions have you taken into consideration in the preparation of the budget?
   e) List critical considerations relevant to stateholders for this project as well as the benefits and costs to the stakeholders if the project is implemented.

CHAPTER 4

CAPITAL EXPENDITURE DECISIONS

4.1 Introduction

Management has a role to play in decision-making about capital expenditures of the organization and therefore must have an understanding of appraisal methods and systems the organization can use. Understanding these methods will help management decide on funds allocation related to capital expenditure decisions. Managers' knowledge of investment appraisal becomes an important tool to enable them to make proper decisions about how the organization can spend its money on capital expenditures.

Investment appraisal is an attempt to assess the financial viability of different investment options that might be available to a business organization. The appraisal is important simply because the company might have different options for investment but is faced with limitations of its financial resources and difficulties in identifying the best option. Under such situations, managers need to apply quantitative techniques to evaluate available options. The appraisal also will help to determine the attractiveness of the various options thus help the managers to make the right decision.

Example of projects that require investment appraisal will be such projects as investment in new cost-saving equipment, investment in new capacities, investment in new premises, marketing campaigns and investments in another firm, merger and acquisition.

4.2 Nature of Investment Appraisal Projects

Investment projects which need to be appraised using quantitative techniques are the ones which qualify to meet the following characteristics:

a. Projects should be long-term in nature
b. They involve long-term commitment of capital sums (the financial investment is large)
c. The decisions to invest in such projects are almost impossible to reverse without accepting a significant loss
d. Since they are involved in the unknown future, such decisions contain an element of uncertainty and can be considered high-risk.
e. Costs are incurred in the present, but benefit occurs in the future.
f. They affect the future profitability of the firm.

4.3 Difference between Long-term decisions and Short-term decisions

It is important to understand that long-term investment decisions are different than short-term investment decisions. Managers need to make proper distinctions between the two so as to weigh the decisions correctly before making long-term investments.

There are major four areas of difference between long and short-term decisions:

a. **Time Span:** Long-term investment decisions have time spans of two years or more while short-term decisions span less than two years.
b. **Focus of the decision:** Long-term projects and decisions are more strategic and focused on the organization's future while short-term investment decisions focus on current organizational concerns.
c. **Financial risk:** The level of spending involved in long-term investment decisions is very large as compared to short-term investment where the level of spending is small or average sized.
d. **External factor consideration:** The consideration of external factors that may impact the organization long term is much more important when making long-term decisions versus short-term decisions.

4.4   Important factors to consider when making investment decisions

Investment decisions are critical to organizations futures. It is therefore very important for managers to consider the unique factors of investment decisions. Understanding of these factors can help managers to make informed and sound investment decisions. These factors are:

1. **Initial cost of the asset**: Managers must know how much money is going to be spent for the project. If the costs are known, managers can begin to plan how to finance the project and where to get funding either through equity financing or debt financing.
2. **The expected benefits from the asset:** This involves the analysis of the expected benefits of the investment in terms of profitability and cash flow.
3. **The operating costs of the investment**: Initial costs of the investment are not enough to make the investment reach the desired objectives if there are not enough funds to cover operating costs during the lifetime of the project.
4. **The expected life of the investment**: This involves the determination of lifetime or the duration of the project so that managers can correctly estimate needed costs over time.
5. **Timing of the benefit**s: This is the projection of timing on the flow of the benefits expected from the investment.
6. **The risk involved:** Every project involves some elements of uncertainty. It is known that projects with higher profits usually carry a higher level of risk; managers must bear this in mind when considering any investment options.
7. **Alternative forms of investment:** Before implementation, project managers should think through alternative investments which are likely to give the same level of benefit so that projects with the greatest benefit with the least financial input can be considered first.
8. **Qualitative as well as quantitative factors**: The quantification of monetary costs and benefits is not the only thing which needs to be weighed. Other qualitative factors such as availability of

market, raw materials and labour must also be considered since project success depends on them.

4.5   Investment Appraisal Methods

In this chapter we will discuss two methods used in appraising investment projects—non-discounting methods and discounting methods.

4.5.1   Non-discounting Methods of Investment Appraisal

Non-discounting methods of investment appraisal will provide criteria for selecting a project from multiple alternative investments available. Each type of non-discounting method, the payback method and the accounting rate of return method, uses different criteria for selecting the best investment. The criteria are based on cash flow or profitability of the project but neither considers the time value of money of the project over its life time. Let's look at these two non-discounting methods of investment appraisal in more detail.

The Payback Method

The payback method considers the time that it takes for the project to recover its initial investment cost as its criteria for project selection. Managers prefer projects in which the payback period of the project is short to those which have a longer payback period. The recovery here is only on the cash flow and does not consider whether the project results in a profit or loss over time. In other words, the payback method is simply the number of years it takes for the project to pay for itself. The payback period can be expressed in number of years or months and it is calculated by adding up annual returns from an investment until the cumulative total equals the initial cost.

Decision Criteria

Under the payback method, the project will be selected among other projects using the following criteria:

1. **Accept the project if** the payback period is less than the target period. The target period is determined by the management
2. **Reject the project if** the payback period is more than the target period.
3. **In the case of competing investment projects,** rank the projects by payback and accept the project with the shortest payback period (provided it meets the target payback period)

Example

Faith Company, Ltd. wishes to invest in one of the three projects below over a period of six years. The expected cash flow of each of the projects are tabulated below. Calculate the payback period of each project. Which project should be selected by Faith Company, Ltd. if the target period is only three years?

Projects cash flow (all figures in United States dollars)

Year	Project A	Project B	Project C
0	(15,000)	(15,000)	(15,000)
1	6,000	4,000	2,000
2	5,000	2,000	8,000
3	4,000	6,000	4,000
3	1,000	3,000	500
5	3,000	3,000	500
6	3,000	2,000	300

Solution
Note: NCF = Net Cash Flows

Years	PROJECT A		PROJECT B		PROJECT C	
	NCF	Cumulative Net flow	NCF	Cumulative Net flow	NCF	Cumulative Net Cash flow
0	-15,000	-15,000	-15,000	-15,000	-15,000	-15,000
1	6,000	-9,000	4,000	-11,000	2,000	-13,000
2	5,000	-4,000	2,000	-9,000	8,000	-5,000
3	4,000	0	6,000	-3,000	4,000	-1,000
4	1,000	1,000	3,000	0	500	-500
5	3,000	4,000	3,000	3,000	500	0
6	3,000	7,000	2,000	5,000	500	500

The payback periods are as follows:

Project A: 3 years   Project B: 4 years   Project C: 5 years

Faith Company, Ltd. should select Project A because it has the shortest payback period compared to other two projects.

Advantages of Payback Method

1. **The payback method is one of the simplest methods to understand and use.** In fact, many individuals in business apply the method without realizing that it is an accounting method of appraising investment opportunities. The application of the payback method doesn't require complex calculations.

2. **The method strongly emphasizes cash flow and the speed of return on the investment.** It recognizes that cash received early is an asset's life, is preferable to cash received later.

3. **It takes into account how quickly the organization recoups its investment**-- short payback means less risk.

4. **The payback method favours projects with an early return.** For an organization with cash flow challenges, an early return is preferred.

5. **Particularly useful when the project life is likely to be short.**

6. **The method can be used as a quick way of screening potential investment projects.**

Disadvantages of Payback Method

1. **The method emphasis is more on cash flow return and ignores the long-term profitability of a project in question.** The major reasons as to why companies do business is to maximize profits. Any investment decisions should consider profit maximization profits as a goal and payback method doesn't consider this idea.

2. **Payback method ignores the timing of cash flow within the and after the payback period.** Even though a project might have good cash flow, if the payback period is higher than the targeted payback period, it will not be considered.

3. **Payback method ignores the time-value of money concept.** The time-value of money assumes that same money today will not have the same value tomorrow. The recovery of the same cash flow in the future ignores this concept.

4. Selecting projects with similar payback period:
   In the instance that projects have similar payback periods,the method does not have other criteria to use to distinguish between these projects hence difficult to select ones among altrnatives

Improvements on the Payback Method

In order to counter some of the disadvantages of the payback method, some improvements have been made in order to incorporate the concept of time-value of money. The future cash flow can easily be discounted before the payback period is calculated. This makes using the payback method in investment appraisal projects more useful though other problems and its limited decision criteria remain the same.

In using discounted cash flow numbers, the payback period will not be the same as when one calculates it using the normal future cash flow. Discounted cash flows tend to increase the payback period and it is difficult determine an exact number of years. The values of future cash flow will never equal the initial investment and so the payback period can not be calculated with absolute certainty. By discounting cash flow, uncertainty and inflation are taken into consideration.

The Accounting Rate of Return

The accounting rate of return method of investment appraisal determines the percentage return that the project achieves over its life time in terms of profitability. The accounting rate of return is simply the relationship between the project investment and the profitability of the investment over its life time. Another term used to describe this relationship is the Average Rate of Return (ARR). ARR expresses annual average profit as a percentage of initial investment over the life of an investment.

The formula to determine ARR is:

$$\text{ARR} = \frac{\text{Average annual profit}}{\text{Average investment}} \times 100$$

The ARR computation is based on anticipated profit rather than forecasted cash flow. The challenge here is in knowing whether to use profit before tax or profits after tax.

Decision Criteria

1. **Accept the project if** the Accounting rate of Return (ARR) is higher than the minimum rate established by the management.
2. **Reject the project if** the Accounting rate of Return (ARR) is less than the minimum rate established by the management
3. **Rank the project as number one if** it has highest Accoiunting rate of return (ARR). The lowest rank will be assigned to the project with the lowest ARR.

Example

Papayas Pty, Ltd. has the following balances in its accounting books at the end of 2007. Opening Stock: $ 10,000, Purchases: $ 20,000, Closing Stock: $ 5,000, Total Sales: $ 50,000, Operating Expenses: $15,000, Current Assets: $ 15,000, Fixed Assets: $ 25,000.

The figure of current assets excludes closing stock. What is the Accounting Rate of Return?

Solution

1. We will need to first calculate the Net Profit as follows:

Sales			$50,000
Cost of Goods Sold			
Opening Stock	$10,000		
Add: Purchases	$20,000		
Goods available for Sale	$30,000		
Less: Closing stock		$5,000	
Cost of Goods Sold			$ 25,000
Gross Profits			$25,000
Operating Expenses			$ 15,000
Net Profit before Tax			**$15,000**

2. We need then need to calculate the Total Assets during the period which is:
   $15,000+ $25,000 + $5,000 = $45,000

   The Accounting rate of return then will be:

   ARR $=$ $\dfrac{\text{Average annual profit}}{\text{Average investment}} \times 100$

   $= \dfrac{\$\ 10,000}{\$\ 45,000} \times 100 = 22.2\%$

4.5.2 Discounting methods of appraising investments

The discounting methods tend to incorporate the time-value of money in calculations by discounting the future cash flow. As future cash flows are discounted, uncertainty and inflation that might affect the future benefits of the investment are taken into consideration. There are two main discounting methods: the Net Present Value (NPV) method and the Internal Rate of Return method.

The Net Present Value (NPV)

The Net Present Value method of investment appraisal takes into consideration the time-value of money concept in the sense that it first discounts the future cash flow of the project and then subtracts these from the initial cost of the investment. The term discounting here means that the future values of the cash flow are reduced to their present value today . By discounting, we assume that money today does not have the same value as money tomorrow. Therefore, as we try to make future investment decisions, we need to bring the future value of the cash flow to the present value (value at the time we are making the decision).

The difference between the initial cost of the investment and the discounted future cash flow is known as the Net Present Value. Once the Net Present Value is calculated, the management can use the NPV to make an informed investment decision (this will be expanded upon later).

Meaning of Discounting

The term discounting in this chapter means reducing future cash flow to their value today. It is the same as the inverse of compounding the present value to obtain future value. Let us first see the meaning of compounding and how to calculate the future value.

Example

Mazuria placed his money in National Bank of Commerce on the 1st of January 2006. He deposited $100,000 and the bank's interest rate was 8% p.a. What will the future value of his investment be after one year?

Solution:

The future value of the investment can be calculated as

$$Fv = Po \, (1 + r)^n$$

Where Fv = Future Value

        Po = Principal Amount

        r = Rate of interest

        n= Time of investment

$= 10,000(1+0.08)^1$

$= \$\ 10,800$

The basic principle of discounting is that if we wish to have $x in a years' time, we need to invest a certain sum less than $x now at the interest rate of r% in order to have the required sum of money by the target date.

By using this future value obtained, we can ask ourselves a question: What is the present value of the $10,800 obtainable after one year?

To obtain the present value means we have to calculate the inverse of the compounding.

$$PV \ = \ \frac{FV}{(1 + r)^n}$$

$$= \ \frac{\$\ 10,800}{(1+0.08)^1}$$

$$= \ \$\ 10,000$$

Calculating the Net Present Value

Net Present Value can be calculated by using the following formula where by future cash flows are discounted on a yearly basis and thereafter the initial investment is deducted.

NPV Formula

$$NPV = \frac{CF_1}{(1+k)^1} + \frac{CF_2}{(1+k)^2} + \frac{CF_3}{(1+k)^3} + ... + \frac{CF_n}{(1+k)^n} - ICO$$

Where:

    NPV = Net Present Values

CFn = the net cash flow receipts at the end of year t

ICO = the initial investment outlay

k = the discount rate / the required minimum rate of return on investment

n = the project / investment duration in years

Example

Masanza Ndagalu Limited intends to invest in a milk processing machine which will cost $75,000. The estimated net cash flow for the next three years are $30,000 in the first year, $37,000 in the second year and $15,000 in the third year. What would be the Net Present Value for this project be if the company's cost of capital is 5%?

Solution

$$NPV = \frac{30,000}{(1+0.05)} + \frac{37,000}{(1+0.05)^2} + \frac{15,000}{(1+0.05)^3} - 75,000$$

$$= \frac{30,000}{1.05} + \frac{37,000}{1.103} + \frac{15,000}{1.16} - 75,000$$

$$= 28,571.43 + 33,544.88 + 12,975.78 - 75,000$$

$$= +89$$

Calculation of Net Present Value by using Present Value Tables

The use of formula in calculating the net present value might seem tedious especially when you have a complex project which involves a large amount of money and a longer period of time. Present Values tables (Discounted Cash Flow Tables) have been developed and tested to help managers calculate Net Present Values without involving themselves in the complex calculations of using the above formula.

Example 1

Using the previous information, we can now easily calculate the Net Present Values of Masanza Ndagalu Ltd as follows:

Years	Cash flow	Discounting Factor (5%)	Present Values
0	(75,000)	1.000	(75,000)
1	30,000	0.952	28,560
2	37,000	0.907	33,559
3	15,000	0.864	12,960

Net Present Value + 79

Note:

The answer obtained through using the table is a bit lower than that obtained when using the table. The difference can be attributed to the approximation of table figure to only three decimal places.

Decisions Criteria for Project Selection

The Net Present Method will select a project whose Net Present Values is positive and will exclude all projects with negative present values. In the case of multiple projects having positive present values, the approach is to rank those projects starting and selecting the ones with highest Net Present Value.

Example 2

NYC Ltd is considering investing its funds in three prospective projects beginning in Jan 2007. The following cash flows at 15% cost of capital are projected in the whole duration periods of these projects. The initial investment for project A is $6,075 and for project B is $7,000. Project A cash flow for the next four years is $2,000, $2,000, $4,000, $3,500. Project B cash flow for the next four years is $3,000, $4,000, $3,500 and $3,000.

Calculate the Net Present Value for each project. Based on the calculations of NPV, which project would you select?

Solution:
Project A

Years	Cash flow	Discounting Factor (5%)	Present Values
0	(6075)	1.000	(6075)
1	2,000	0.870	1,740
2	3,000	0.756	2,268
3	3,000	0.658	1,974
4	4,000	0.572	2,288

Net Present Value + 2195
Project B

Years	Cash flow	Discounting Factor (5%)	Present Values
0	(7000)	1.000	(7,000)
1	3,000	0.870	2,610
2	4,000	0.756	3,024
3	3,500	0.658	2,303
4	3,000	0.572	1,716

Net Present Value + 2,653

The project which should be selected is Project B because of its higher net present value

Advantages of Net Present Value Method

1. The calculation of net present value **takes into consideration of time-value of money.**
2. The method **takes into account the profitability of the projects over its life time.**

3. **All cash flow during the lifetime of the project is taken into consideration** while in payback period methods only cash flow within the payback period is taken into account.

Disadvantages of Net Present Value Method

1. The calculations of Net Present Value are **difficult and complex.**
2. The interpretation is **easily misunderstood**
3. **The determination of cost of capital can be done arbitrarily and may be subjective.**

The Internal Rate of Return

The Internal Rate of Return (IRR) is the rate of return which will give the Net Present Value equal to zero. In order to arrive at that rate, the present value of future cash inflow should be equal to the present value of cash outflow. The calculation of IRR is done by trial and error until you obtain a discount rate that gives a net present value of zero. In case the answer does not give as the NPV which equals to zero, then we can keep trying but it may be very tedious. **Calculation of IRR where there is unequal cashflow is very challenging as you have to do by trial and error until you have the IRR that gives you NPV equals to Zero**

The formula for calculation of IRR is determined as:

$$IRR \ = \ NPV \ = \ \Longrightarrow 0$$

$$NPV = \frac{CF_1}{(1+k)^1} + \frac{CF_2}{(1+k)^2} + \frac{CF_3}{(1+k)^3} + \ldots + \frac{CF_n}{(1+k)^n} - ICO$$

Where:

CFn = the Net Cash flow receipts at the end of year n

ICO = the Initial Investment Outlay

k = the discount rate / the required minimum rate of return on investment

n = the project / investment duration in years

Calculating the IRR where there is unequal cash flow

Example

ABC Ltd is considering an investment in a modern juice processing plant at initial costs of $16,000. The expected cash inflow for the first year is $ 8,000, for the second year is $8,600 for the second year and $6,000 for the third year. The cost of capital is estimated at 10%.

Calculate the Internal Rate of Return.

Solution:

Calculation of internal return can be done by trial and error method:

Step 1

The IRR is rate which leads to NPV equivalent to Zero.
Obtaining that rate let us try k = 20 % and see what will be the NPV
NPV = 8, 000(0.833) + 7,000(0.694) + 6,000(0.579)-16,000
   = - 1,004
A negative NPV of $ -1,004 at 20% indicates that the project's true rate is lower than 20%

Step 2

From the previous calculations we have seen that the true rate cannot be 20%. Let us try another rate of 16% and see what the Net Present Value will be.

NPV = 8,000(0.862) +7,000(0.743) +6000(0.641)-16,000
   = -57
Again the NPV is not equivalent to zero although it is very near to zero. Probably if we try another figure below 16%, we can get closer to zero.

Step 3

Let us try 15 % as a rate for discount
NPV = 8,000(0.870) + 7,000(0.756) + 6000(0.658) -16,000
      = 200

The trial and error method can be tiring and, again, it will not provide an exact rate that will give us a project NPV which is equivalent to zero. In order to give an approximately correct answer, we will need to use the Linear Interpolation Method.

Step 4

The true rate of return should lie between 15% and 16%. We can therefore find out a close approximation of the rate of return by the method of linear interpolation as follows.

	Present Value	Difference
Present Value Required	16,000	
		200
Present Value at Lowest Rate 15%	16,200	
		257
Present Values at Higher Rate 16%	15,943	

$$IRR = 15\% + (16-15) \text{ X } \frac{200}{257}$$

= 15%+0.80 = 15.8%

Approximately IRR = 16%

Calculating IRR when you have equal Cash Flows

When you have equal cash flow, this means you have a fixed amount paid or received at a future specified date. This is an annuity. The computation of IRR becomes a little bit easier when cash flow is equal than when you have unequal cash flow of mixed streams.

Example

Tarime Ltd has an investment that would cost $200,000 and would provide an annual cash inflow of $54,300 for the next 6 years with 10% cost of capital. What is the Internal Rate of Return?

Solution:

IRR can be found as follows:

NPV= - 200,000 + 54300(PVAF6 k) = 0
200,000=54,300 (PVAF$_{6,}$ k)
PVAF6, k = $\frac{200,000}{54,300}$

= 3.683

The rate which gives a PVAF6 of 3.683 for 6 years is the project's internal rate of return. Looking up PVAF in a table across the 6 year row, we find an approximately correct number under the 16% column. Therefore the IRR will be 16%

Profitability index

Some investment situations require a choice between alternative investments or options to achieve one particular objective. There are two ranking techniques based on discounting methods of appraisal and each has a particular role to play.

The profitability index is the name given to this measurement:

Profitability Index = $\frac{\text{NPV of Inflows}}{\text{Capital Invested}}$

Example

Masala Kulagwa intends to buy a juice making machine at a cost $30,000. The expected cash inflow of the machine for each of the next five years is $9,000. The cost of capital is 10%. Calculate the profitability index.

Solution:

Year	Cash Flow	DCF (10%)	Present Value
0	-30,000	1.000	(30,000)
1	9000	0.909	8,181
2	9000	0.826	7,434
3	9000	0.751	6,759
4	9000	0.683	6,147
5	9000	0.621	5,589
		NPV=	**+4,110**

Calculation of Profitability Index

Profitability Index = $\dfrac{\text{NPV of Inflows}}{\text{Capital Invested}}$

= $\dfrac{\$ 34,110}{\$ 30,000}$

= 1.13

Projects with higher profitability indexes will be selected. The normal benchmark is 1. Any project with profitability index that is less than 1 should not be selected.

4.6   Conclusion

These topics may be eye openers for Chief Executive Officers and managers on how they should move forward with long-term investment decisions related to capital expenditures. The topics have explained different methods to use when making decisions about investment options. The methods discussed in this chapter are more quantitative in nature but they are not to be applied in isolation of qualitative factors which may have direct impact on the investment choices.

Practice Questions

Question 1

  (a) Discuss the concept of investment appraisal and popular methods used for such appraisal in a typical business enterprise.
  (b) What are the main characteristics of capital investment decisions?

Question 2

An underground rapid transport system is being considered for your country's capital city. Who are likely to be the key stakeholders? What are the respective costs and benefits? Discuss.

Question 3

The Ministry of Transport is considering starting an underground rail system in your country in order to eliminate fleet road congestion. The funding of the project has not yet been identified but there are donors who are interested in funding the project. The Ministry has approached you to be one of the project team members. The terms of reference given to the project team are given below:

  (a) Enumerate the Project objectives and goals; identify all possible project activities that are likely to take place during the implementation of the project.
  (b) List what considerations key stakeholders may have in this project. What are likely to be the benefits and costs to the stakeholders?
  (c) Prepare a budget based on the activities you have identified above. Include the assumptions that you have taken into consideration in your budget preparation.
  (d) Advice the ministry how to go about sourcing funds for the budget you have prepared. As a Team leader of the project write a comprehensive report to the Ministry taking into considerations the issues raised in the terms of reference including the estimated budget for the project.

Question 4

"Investment appraisal in non-profit organizations is the same as investment appraisal in profit making business enterprises". Do you agree? Why or why not? Choose an organization you are interested in and evaluate the approaches that have been used over the past years for investment appraisal and examine the limitations, if any, of the approaches in times of uncertainty.

Question 5

A&A Company Ltd is considering purchasing a brick-making machine. The expected life time of the machine is 5 years with depreciation amount of $10,000 per year. The projection for sales of bricks in year 1 are $24,000, year 2 $22,000, year 3 $25,000, year 4 $17,000 and year 5 $20,000. Projected direct costs are $4,000 for year 1 and thereafter they are expected to increase by 8% per year. The cost of capital is 12%.

Required

1. Calculate the Accounting Rate of Return
2. Calculate the Net Present Value of the Machine
3. Would you advise the company to invest in this machine?

CHAPTER 5

PUBLIC SECTOR INVESTMENT DECISIONS

5.1 Introduction

Investment appraisal in the public sector is slightly different from the approaches we have already discussed in the previous chapter. The private sector investor is more concerned with profitability and other costs and benefits which cannot be quantified in monetary values are not a part of the appraisal process.

With this notion in mind, investment appraisal for the public sector must go beyond traditional methodologies of appraising projects and must supplement the traditional methods with social cost benefit analyses.

Social cost benefit analysis will consider other costs and benefits which cannot be quantified in monetary terms. These costs and benefits have impact on stakeholders and so they are important to consider before embarking on any public sector investment . Under social cost benefit methods, there are three analyses that must be conducted before selecting a project. These analyses are in addition to the traditional investment appraisal methods explained in the previous chapter.

Economic Analysis

This involves analyzing the total impact of the project to the overall economy. Economic appraisal adjusts costs and benefits to determine the costs and benefits to the economy at large rather than only to the project.

Indirect effects of the project that are not easily captured by the price mechanism are also noted.

Financial Analysis

This analysis will examine the financial cash flow that will be generated by the project itself and the direct costs/cash outflow of the project measured at market prices. The cash outflow will include the initial costs of the investments and all running costs of the projects. Cash inflow generated will include the net revenues generated by the project during its life time.

Social Costs Benefits Analysis

This involves the analysis of the total positive and negative impact of the project to all stakeholders. Normally, in this case, we are talking about non-financial costs and benefits which the project is likely to bring when implemented. Social costs benefit analysis is often viewed as equivalent to the net present value method used in evaluating private investments but this method also examines the distributional consequences of particular project choices.

5.2 Investment Appraisal by International funding organizations

The investment appraisal for projects funded by international donor organizations such as the World Health Organization (WHO) World Bank, and others, includes a close look at how projects selected will contribute to the welfare of the country.

The investment appraisal by these organizations goes beyond issues traditionally covered by a standard cost benefit analysis. The economic analysis for projects funded by international donors must include answers to the following questions:

1. What is the objective of the project?
2. What will change if the project is implemented? What if it's not?
3. Is this particular project the best choice to meet the goals?

4. Are there any separable components in the project? 5. Who are the winners and losers if this project is implemented?

5. Is the project financially sustainable after funding ends?

6. What is the project's fiscal impact?

7. What is the project's environmental impact?

8. Is the project worthwhile?

9. What risks does the project entail?

Other factors that will be considered under economic analysis will be the borrowing conditions of the country, fiscal policy of the country and funding priorities of the donor institution. The decision criteria for investment selection are very tricky in these cases: traditional NPV and IRR methods will be used but, to avoid unplanned projects or imposed projects by higher authorities without proper investment analysis, these criteria are not used in the final appraisal.

The investment appraisal also must include:

1. **Benefit estimation**: normally considers whether there are the aggregate benefits to the country

2. **Cost estimation**: of the project based on domestic prices.

3. **Environmental impact assessments**

4. **Risk Mitigation**: This is the analysis of risks that are likely to affect the project and possible mitigation options

5. **Evaluation of the fiscal impact** of the project: The reason for this evaluation is to ensure that the impact of project on the country is sustainable

6. **Project running costs**: It must be established whether the running costs will be ensured throughout the period of the project.

7. **Evaluation of private participation on financing**: Donors will require information about any private contributors to the project.

8. **Distributional impacts**: of projects focusing on issues such as poverty alleviationand services improvement in industries such as health and education.

5.3   Conclusion

The use of traditional quantitative techniques in appraising private sector investments has not changed much over the last decade. We know that quantatitave techniques which include the non-discounting and discounting methods are widely used in public sector projects but these methods are not ideal for these project types . Managers have to adopt a different approach for donor-funded projects and invest time in considering and outlining the concerns of all project stakeholders in terms of the project social costs and benefits --not only financial and economic impact.

Practice Questions

Question 1

Explain the meaning of social costs and social benefits and give relevant examples which may come up in the construction of a public hospital.

Question 2

Discuss how international organizations would appraise development projects in your country. Give a concrete example of a project that has been recently funded by an international organization.

Question 3

What major problems are managers likely to face when preparing project feasibility studies ?

CHAPTER 6

CRISIS MANAGEMENT

6.1   Introduction

In normal operations of both for-profit and non-profit organizations, the uncertainty and risk cannot be full avoided. The level of uncertainty from one organization to another may differ beacuse of differences in the nature of operations, the environment surrounding the organization or for other reasons.

There are various types, causes, and possible area of risk which impact organizations differently. One must consider, however, that there is a clear relationship between risk and crisis. In some cases, crises are considered to be the major risk factor so clarifying the relationship between risk and crisis in this chapter is very important.

Risk Management is of utmost importance and management must understand how to effectively manage risks to minimize negative impact on the organizations they are leading. When risks are not properly managed, they are likely to affect organizational operations and may result in major financial loss or other social costs. No organization can escape impacts of unmanaged risks so effective risk management knowledge and skills should be sought out and valued. Managers must be able to identify, analyze, and evaluate risk, and also then must create a risk mitigation plan. Some risks can be easily predicted but risks arising from crises are unpredictable. Regardless of the type of risk, though, all risks need to be mitigated whenever possible.

6.2   Definition of a crisis

A crisis is an unexpected event that is likely to have a negative impact on the well-being of an organization. A crisis will likely bring disruption to the organizational operations which may impact customers, employees, production capacities or other areas. When a crisis occurs, both present and future operations may be seriously impacted. Crises create risk to the organization, its employees, production capacity, community relatinoships and stakeholders. Anyone or any organization who has a direct relationship with the organization may feel the impact of the crisis.

Crises vary from fairly predictable crises to totally unexpected crises such as the 2010 volcanic eruption in Iceland which impacted the Kenyan flower industry. When volcanic ash appeared, airlines could not fly and airports were temporarily closed for days. This crisis negatively impacted the transportation of flowers from Kenya to the world market, for example. Such type of the crisis was totally unexpected and little preparation for a crisis of this type could be made.

6.3   Types of crises

There are many types of crises, all of which cannot be explained here, but, for the purpose of better understanding, we will group crises into several broad groups with descriptions of crises which may fall into these groups. The following are important groups of crises to consider when looking at risks to an organization:

a.   **Natural disasters (often referred to as 'Acts of God')** : Natural disasters are beyond human control. They include physical destruction from floods, earthquakes, tornadoes, etc.

b.   **Industrial Accidents:** Industrial accidents include man-made disasters caused by construction collapses, fires, release of toxic chemicals or fumes, oil spills, etc.

c.   **Public Relations Crises:** Public relations crises occur industrial strikes, pressure from political groups, unwelcomed media attention, adverse media publicity and/or removal or loss of CEO or other key management. These crises damage the image of the organization.

d. **Business and Management Crises:** These crises can be caused by sudden workforce strikes in your organization or that of a key supplier, the loss of a major customer, a competitor launching a new product or a sudden shortfall in demand for a company's product

e. **Legal Crises**: Legal crises can result from a product liabililty such as a company being taken to court by customers as a result of an injury or health care problems, employees suing the company or fraud committed by organizational employees which results to court cases.

All these type of crises create risk to the organization and can have tremendous effects on the operation of the organization.

6.4   Crisis Management

Crises cannot always be avoided but they must managed in an organized and efficient way to minimize negative impact to the organization. Crisis management involves identifying a crisis, planning a response, responding to a events that pose a significant threat to the firm, limiting damage, and creating and training an individual and team to deal with and resolve the crisis. The following recommendations suggest an efficient way of handling a crisis situation at the organizational level:

a. **Appoint a crisis manager and crisis management team:** The crisis manager is an intergal party in the process of handling a sudden crisis. The crisis manager will be responsible for event tracking, management of human resources, damage assessment, development of contingency plans, assessing resources and options, coordinating external bodies and managing and coordinating communication during and after the crisis. The crisis management team will support the crisis manager to plan and handle risks events.

b. **Put in place a crisis management plan**: Management should plan ahead so that they know what to do in the event of a crisis. Organizations that experience drastic and extreme negative impacts from crises usually have failed to develop a crisis management plan in advance. A strong crisis management plan helps management designate specific actions to use in case a crisis occurs in the future.

c. **Objectively assess causes and effects of a crisis:** Determine whether the causes will have a long-term or short-term effect on the organization and focus on what can be done to mitigate or eliminate the problems created by the crisis.

d. **Designate one person to speak about the crisis to the outside world**: One person will be chosen to address different individuals or corporate entities that require information about the crisis. Choosing the wrong person may aggrevate the crisis or result in the result of incorrect information. The chosen person must be prepared to respond effectively to questions related to crisis issues as asked by stakeholders, journalists, and politicians.

e. **Dealing with negative information:** Management should act quickly to prevent or counter the spread of negative information about the crisis

f. **Use of Media:** When possible and needed, utilize the media to provide a positive counter argument to that which may be negatively reported by individuals or groups.

g. **Stick to the truth and avoid partial truths:** trying to manipulate or distort information may backfire and create additional problems for your organization. Speak clearly and succinctly.

6.5 Stages in Crisis Management

Whether predictable or unpredictable, crises tend to move through the following stages:

a. **Warning indicators** may be present prior to a crisis. These indicators show that there is or could be an event liable to cause a significant impact to the organisation in the near future.

b. **The crisis point** occurs when the event begins to cause significant impact on the organization. The crisis point may happen at any time so a contingency plan should always be in place.

c. **Recovery** comes after the acute stage of crisis has passed and the organization is able to focus on returning to normal operations.

d. **Post-crisis Evaluation** of the effects of the crisis help the organization repair damages to the organization

6.6   Conclusion

There are many situations in normal business life which can trigger a crisis situation and increase risk to an organization. This chapter has tried to define what crisis is and has briefly highlighted possible causes of risk in an organization . The topic explains also the different types of risks and the stages in crisis management . Futher more, it gives various recommendations on how management can apply different methods to ensure proper handling a crisis situations at the organizational level.

Practice Questions

Question 1

Identify a crisis event in your organization that happened within the last year or so. Discuss what the major causes and consequences of the crisis were to your organization. Make a contingency plan for your organization which will help your organization minimize or mitigate the consequences of re-occurance of a similar crisis. What may challenge your ability to implement this plan?

Question 2

Discuss how management can be proactive in mitigating the negative impacts of crises for their organizations.

Question 3

Explain in details the stages in crisis management . What do you think should be done at each stage of a crisis?

CHAPTER 7

RISK MANAGEMENT

7.1   Definition of Risk

There is no single, universal definition of the term 'risk'. Risk can be defined as a degree of uncertainty or could include uncertainties as part of the definition of risk. There are many definitions so we have selected a few to give a general understanding of the term:

a.   The possibility of incurring misfortune or loss;
b.   A threat that an event, action or failure to act will adversely affect an organization's ability to achieve its business objectives and execute its strategies effectively;
c.   A change that will impact the meeting of objectives.

Definitions which exclude uncertainties from risk are based on the argument that risk is the chance or probability of danger, loss, injury or other adverse consequence while uncertainties are unknown, unreliable, ever-changing or erratic. The other main difference between risks and uncertainties is that with risks, a measure of probability can be attached to the various outcomes while in the case of uncertainties, the probability of an event happening is too vague and is impossible to quantify.

7.2   Risk Management

Risk Management is an integrated program for prevention, monitoring, and control of areas of potential liability exposure. The responsibility of developing such programs lays in the hands of organizational management. Risk Management seeks to prevent liability through a process of education, feedback, and early response.

Managing risk enables organizations to achieve their potential with the least chance of risk interference. Effective risk management also enables managers to take advantage of opportunities as they arise and minimise the barriers to meeting our business objectives through the application of different strategies to mitigate risks which may occur over time. The strategies may differ from one organization to another; there is not one strategy to mitigate all types of risks.

Risk management is a central part of any organisation's strategic planning and management. It is the process whereby organizations methodically address the risks attached to their activities with the goal of sustained benefit from each and every activity. Good risk management identifies and addresses risks. Its objective is to add maximum sustainable value to all the activities of the organization. It marshals the understanding of the potential upside and downside of all those factors which can affect the organization. It increases the probability of success, and reduces both the probability of failure and the uncertainty of achieving the organization's overall objectives. (BOT Risk Management Guidelines, 2005).

7.3   Scope of Risk Management

The scope of risk management is the extent to which the organization can plan for and protects against risks to the organization. Under normal circumstances, organizations should define its scope of risk management on its risk management policy. The scope should include all events which are likely to pose risks to the organization's operations. Risks such as fires, accidents, theft and outbreak of diseases, among many others, should be outlined in the risk management plan.

7.4   Risk Management Process

Risk management is a process rather than a one-off for no other reason than there are new areas of risks everyday. When a manager tries and succeeds in managing one risk, he or she cannot be sure that this risk will not occur again or that they will be successful in managing it in the future.. The process of risk management should include,

- *Establishing goals and context*

    Effective risk management in any organization requires a thorough understanding of the context in which the organization operates. The context sets the scope for the risk management process and includes strategic, organisational and risk management considerations. The context will also define the relationship between the organization and its environment.

- *Risk Identification*

    In order to manage risks, the organization or corporation must identify existing and future risks by considering current and future business ventures as well as any potential new business initiatives. Risk identification should be a continuous process and should occur at both the transaction and portfolio level.

- *Evaluation and Measurement*

    Once risks have been identified, they should be measured in order to determine their impact on the organization operations. This can be done using various techniques ranging from simple to sophisticated models. Accurate and timely measurement of risk is essential to effective risk management systems. Organizations which do not have a risk measurement system have limited ability to control or monitor risk levels. It is very important that from time to time, organizations test to make sure that the measurement tools it uses are accurate.

7.5   Possible areas of risk

The areas where risks can happen in a business or non-profit organization vary but the following are possible in most businesses, often caused by political or business reasons:

- ▶ Financial Risks
- ▶ Reputation Risks
- ▶ Fraud and Integrity Risks
- ▶ Disasters Risks
- ▶ Crises
- ▶ Malpractice
- ▶ Violence
- ▶ Health Related Risks

7.6   Responding to Risks

Response to risks will depend completely on the type of risks involved. The Chief Executive, together with the management team, should not respond to any risks event wihout proper understanding of the nature and causes of the risks. There are different options of dealing with risks depending on the type of risk you are dealing with. One of the options of dealing with the risk is to transfer the risk. In this case, you can consider transferring the risks to others through methods such as purchasing insurance against theft or fire. You can also accommodate risks. You can only accommodate those type of risks which are likely not having any negative impact or less risks to the organization. Lastly companies can try to avoid risks by not enganging in any business which can pose high risks to the organization. Chief Executive Officers and managers can also avoid risks by not taking any decisions which can lead the organization to incur huge losses, reduce company profitability or market shares.

7.7   Stakeholders analysis and involvement in risk management

Stakeholders are individuals or groups of people who have direct involvement with the organizations and who are likely to be indirect or directly impacted by risk occurances. In organizations, stakeholders include customers, staff, suppliers, government and its agencies, lenders, donors, and shareholders. The role of minimizing and mitigating risks in organizations should not involve only the management but all stakeholders so a broad assessment of risks can be created.

Stakeholder analysis involves indentifying all individuals, groups or organizations who are likely to be affected by the consequences of a risk occurance. Stakeholders involvement provides opportunity to all these parties to get involved in the process of indentifying, minimizing and mitigating risks through effective planning. Stakeholders involvement provides a wider perspective to the management on how to identify possible areas of risk and to evaluate them and design proper strategies for mitigation.

Stakeholders analysis can also be used to ensure that:

- There is proper identification of people, groups and institutions that are likely to have positive or negative influence in risk management and mitigation strategies
- Proper risk management strategies are developed and implemented as planned

Since causes of risks vary from one organization to another and they can occur in and between all levels, stakeholder involvement will help management to plan for a wide range of risks.

7.8   Why should stakeholders be involved in risks management?

Stakeholders involment in risk management is important to the organization for the following reasons

1. Stakeholders should be sensitized on all possible areas of risk to the organization which are likely to have a negative impact on the organization

2. The involvement will help stakeholders identify other possible areas of risks and their causes thus helping management plan for these in advance
3. It helps in identifying the roles which each key stakeholder is likely to play in mitigating organizational risks
4. It helps stakeholders to get involved in mitigating organizational risks
5. It helps to define the involvement of each individual or group stakeholders in each possible area of risk

7.9 Areas of stakeholder involvement

The areas of involvement of stakeholders by companies will be differentiated by various levels in the organization. In some areas of involvement, for example, only senior management are likely to be involved while other employees may need to be involved in other areas. The following are common areas of stakeholder involvement in risk management:

a. Involvement in risk management policy design
b. Involvement in the risk-planning stage
c. Training and sensitization on possible areas of risk
d. Identification of possible areas of risk to the organization
e. Designing strategies for mitigating risks on identified areas of risks

7.10 Conclusion

Risk Management is a very broad subject that cannot be covered in just one chapter but we hope this has increased your general knowledge of the subject. It is also becoming a profession in and of itself and so organizations should employ specialists manage organizational risks effectively and efficiently. This chapter, briefly gives the definition of risk management, explains the scope of risk management and the process of risk management. It further explains how managementment should responding to risks and the reasons as to why management should involve stakeholders in risk management and the areas of involvement.

Practice Questions

Question 1

Select one organization in your country and two areas of potential risk to the organization and conduct risk management identification, analysis, and evaluation to determine the risks treatment in your scenario. What limitations are likely to impair your risk mitigation techniques?

Question 2

Morogoro Teachers College in Tanzania offers a diploma course. The diploma course is for two years and the students come from all parts of Tanzania. The college is built on a large unfenced plot which allows people to come onto the campus without prior notification. The college employs private security guards but they do not carry modern security equipment.

At the beginning of the first term, all students are required to pay their school fees to the college account by cash before they allowed to attend classes. This has been the practice for the last four years with no negative outcomes. This year, however, thieves came into the cash office and set off explosives in the college cashier's office, the safe and the principal's office. Unfortunately, the bandits managed to escape with more than $15,000 in cash, which was the all the money collected on that day. The cashier and the college principal sustained minor injuries and one security guard was killed when he tried to stop the thieves as they left.

- What are the main causes of this event?
- What are likely impacts of this scenario to the college?
- Which measures should the school management take in order to minimize the risk of the reoccurance of this event in the future?
- What are likely to be the limitations in implementing the risk management strategies?

Question 3

Student violence poses major risks to the normal operation of schools and colleges. Recently, Tarime Teachers College experienced high stress and a a tense environment due to student violence which caused insecurity to the college community, damage to school property and loss of classtime for college students. A problem assessment team was formed to identify the causes of the violence as well the impact and effective strategies to mitigate the stress and to prevent future occurances of student violence on campus.

a. Establish possible causes of student violence, the impact of this violence and strategies to mitigate the risks as part of the elected committee.
b. Discuss how the school management can incorporate the recommendations of the committee in their existing risk management policy.

CHAPTER 8

RISK MANAGEMENT POLICY

8.1 Introduction

Designing a risk management policy for any organization is a cornerstone for minimizing negative impact arising from risk. Risk management policies should be designed for the purposes of providing guidelines on how organizations can identify, measure, monitor and control risks that may arise during normal organizational operations.

8.2 The importance of Having a Risk Management Policy

Designing a risk management policy for your organization should not be optional but seen as a necessary mechanism for dealing with risk. Management should be proactive in safeguarding the organization against risk exposure events. The following are some reasons which emphasize the importance of having a risk management policy:

a. Risk management policies provide a guideline on how management should approach risk in their organizations and minimize the impact of risk to the organization operations,

b. Risk management policies help management ensure that all staff are involved in making decisions about risk mitigation.

A clear and relevant policy allows staff to be easily involved in decision- making,

c. The simple existance of risk management policy creates a systematic procedure for use in managing various risks to the organization,

d. It guides development of strategic plans for risk management,

e. The policy creates room for new ideas for improvement,

f. It improves channels of communication, and

g. Helps to reduce costs in terms of time, finances, and resources.

8.3 Factors to consider when designing a risk management policy

The sucesss of any risk management policy depends on a number of issues related to the specific organization designing the policy. The following are some factors which should be considered when designing a risk management policy:

a. **Nature of business:** Risks management policy depends so much on the nature of the business undertaken by the company and the business environment

b. **Availablity of resources: Resources availablity enhances the implementation of the risk management policy.**Inadequate resources may impair the implementation of the policy.

c. **Human resources availability play a major role in implementing risk management policy.**

d. **Business environment:**
   The location of the organization and surrounding environment may influence what goes into an organization's risk management plan

e. **Environment considerations:**
   Location, staff, call board, infrastructure, etc.

f. **Government policies:**
   Education, health, and other policies may be referenced in the risk management plan

g. **Possible organization specific risks:**
   • Employee expertise: For example, if you have fire experts on staff, utilize their expertise in your fire prevention plans

- Communication mechanisms
- Risk Management team should be focused on minimizing clashes in decision making, and bringing a sense of ownership. The management team should consist of college board, students representatives, staff members, community leaders, political leaders.

8.4   Developing a Risk Management Policy

In designing a risk management policy, the involvement of various stakeholders is important so as to be able to address all areas of possible risk all respective areas of the organization. The Chief Executive Officer is the primary leader and overseer of all matters concerning the institution.

Variables of Risk Management policy

These are key issues which must be included in any risk management policy. These will provide guidelines for how management should approach risk management issues. The variables in the risk management policy may include the preamble, objectives of the policy, scope of the policy, roles and responsibilities, risk management procedures and conclusion.

Preamble

This section gives a brief introduction of what the policy contains. The section should include the purpose of the policy and will give clear information on who owns the risk management policy.

Policy Objectives

This section should clearly state the objectives intended by the policy and should stipulate how these objectives will be achieved . Policy objectives could include,for example: creating awareness of the necessity of risk management, safeguarding the organization against loss or destruction, and how to deal with damages resulting from a risk

The policy may also state how the organization will achieve its policy objectives such as through creating clear roles, responsibilities, and reporting mechanisms in the organization related to risk management, having clear and open lines of communication and monitoring mechanisms of risk-related issues.

Scope of the policy

This section should give a description of the key issues that the policy will address. It will define and explain the boundaries that management should operate within when addressing risks issues in the organization.

Roles and Responsibilities

This section will specify who is responsible for risk management activities for the organization. The section must define how each of the designated officers should be involved in the risk management process. The policy should state how the Board of Directors, Chief Executive Officers and other members of management should be involved .

Risk Management Procedure

In the risk management proceudre section, the procedures to be carried out in the event of a risk occurance should be explained in detail. From procedures related to establishing risk context to risk identification, analysis and evaluation and finally to risk treatment, the more detail included, the more prepared the organization will be in the event of an emergency. This section should also stipulate the procedures which will be used to monitor and review risk and how communication about risk occurrences will be communicated internally and externally to stakeholders and others.

8.5   Conclusion

Risk Management is a broad subject that cannont be disccussed in fully in just one or two chapters. The author would encourage managers who are directly involved in risk management of their organizations, and especially those who would like a career in risk management, to pursue professional credentialing in risk management. This will equipt them with more knowledge in risk management so they are better able to manage complex risk management situations effectively.

Practice Question

Question 1

Chilonwa Teacher's College is a college situated in Northern Tanzania. The college was opened in 1980 and, since then, it has been operating successfully. The college offers a diploma course in teaching which requires two years of study. The college provides accomodation for the majority of its students but a few live off-campus.

Recently, a number of crises have been reported by the college Academic Officer that threaten the reputation of the college and impact its normal operations. These crises also threaten the ability of the college to achieve its objective of preparing qualified and competent teachers. These crises include theft, strikes, drug abuse and disease among students. The causes of these crises, according to the Academic Officer include: poor food quality, lack of quality teaching and learning supplies, poverty, unethical behaviours and an uninspiring learning environment. The cause of student strikes was identified as negative student attitudes and disappointment among members of staff in regards to food quality and poor social and economic backgrounds.

Several steps have been taken to curb these problems but with little success. Some of these steps included warning responsible staff and students about future consequences of their behaviours, provision of guidance and couselling services to students, improving teacher training, improving the school enviornment and engaging students in other economic activities to supplement their college budgets.

Required:

From this scenario, develop a risk management policy to help the management to mitigate risks and prevent the same challenges from occurring again.

CHAPTER 9

MANAGEMENT OF POLITICAL RISKS

9.1 Introduction

Political risks arise when a local company extends its operation from its home country to a foreign country for trade or investment. It is very common for multi-national organizations and trans-national corporations from developed countries to move operations to less-developed countries. Most of the time the reason for the shift is to save money by shifting production centres to countries with cheap labour and where there is a market for their products. Many companies who operate in more than one country face political risks that, at times, lead to confiscation of their investment with or without compensation from the host country.

Political risk is defined as governmental or societal actions and policies, originating either within or outside the host country, that negatively affect either a select group of, or the majority of, foreign business operations and investments. Political risk arise because sovereign country can change laws and regulations as they choose and those impacted by these changes may not have any recourse. Sometimes political risks arise from host country government actions intending to push foreign investors out from the country.

Another common political risk is referred to as "creeping expropriation" whereby a government decides to add tax to an investment or change laws or regulations knowing that these changes will have a direct negative impact on the project. In practice, governments change tax rules, royalties and contracts at will which increases the level of uncertainty faced by foreign companies operating in other countries.

There are numbers of examples of political risks worldwide that showcase foreign investors' assets and properties being confiscated as a result of their host country's decision. In 1967, Tanzania embarked on a socialist policy which required nationalizing all private properties of both foreign investors and local investors without compensation. In Uganda, there was also a move by the government to force foreign investors out the country and confiscate their investments under Iddi Amin's rule as president. To re-attract foreign investors, these countries have worked to return properties to their original owners after many years of negotiation.

Another recent example of political risk in Africa came through Zimbabwe. A number of years ago, the Zimbabwe government decided to take over all farms owned by foreign investors and distributed them to locals, a move which was condemned by Britain and other foreign countries. There was no compensation for the original owners who had already invested in and developed their farms. Zimbabwe ignored all complaints about the decisions to nationalize the farms and continued with the political agenda they had set. The case of Zimbabwe may differ slightly as there seemed to be evidence of agreements that those farmers were to be compensated by Britain but either way, the political risk was huge to all foreign farm owners.

The democratic movement across the globe has now minimized some political risks as countries are forced to consider human rights and the protection of foreign investors. A country which does not consider human rights is viewed negatively in the global economy and foreign investors are discouraged from investing money in such countries. To attract foreign investors, countries comply with a number of clauses related to human rights as stipulated by various international organizations and conventions.

The dimension of political risks is not restricted to confiscation of properties by host countries, though, but is rather extended to include the impact of international terrorism activities which are likely to directly impact foreign investors' properties. Other manifestations of political risks includes restrictions on maximum ownership of shares by foreigners, restrictions on property ownership by foreigners, nationalization and control of local operations.

9.2   Categories of Political Risks

According to Hamada and Haugerudbraaten (2004), political risk takes three dimensions and include expropriation, transfer, and political violence risks.

a.   **Expropriation risk** refers to losses due to measures taken or approved by the host government that deprive the investor of its ownership or control over its investment, or, in the case of debt, result in the project enterprise being unable to meet its obligations to the lender.

b.   **Transfer risk** refers to the inability to convert local currency (capital, interest, profits, royalties, and other remittances) into foreign currency for transfer outside the host country.

c.   **Political violence risk** refers to losses from damage to, or the destruction or disappearance of, tangible assets because of politically motivated acts of war or civil disturbance in the host country. These acts may include revolutions, insurrections, *coups d'état*, sabotage, or terrorism. Political violence risk can cause an interruption in project operations which results in an unviable project or an inability to fulfil obligations to lenders.

9.3   Causes of Political Risks

There are several causes of political risks which the Chief Excutive officers and managers who manage international business must know . Understanding the factors causing political conflicts will help managers in their decision of doing international business.

a.   ***Civil and ethnic fighting or war***

Civil wars in Africa are common causes of political risks which have direct impact to foreign business operations. In Northern Uganda, Sudan,The Democratic Republic of Congo, Rwanda and Burundi, recent civil wars have negatively impacted both local and foreign investments. Another example of business being impacted by civil fighting occurred in 2009 in Kenya immediately after the election. Political havoc posed high risk to investors in Kenya at that time.

b. *Terrorism*

The use of suicide attacks and other terrorist violence has drastically increased the threat of damage to business investments from terrorism. Example of terrosim previous bombing attacts in some Countries such as Tanzania and Kenya shows how such events are determintal to countries economic infrastucture.

c. *Democratic Transitions*

With the growing trend towards democratization, governments have experienced numerous shifts in power. These changes have occurred more in Africa because there were fewer countries with democratic governments. The change of government systems and of individual power holders has resulted in risks to multi-national corporations because some governments have refused to honour original agreements established between the prior government and the corporation. While more common in Africa, these risks have also been found in Russia, Hungary, and Ecuador.

d. *Resistance from local firms*

Foreign investors are likely to face challenges of political risks caused by stronger local firms especially when foreign investors create strong competition for the local firms. Many local firms in developing countries have been operating as monopolies and the entrance of competitive foreign companies may not be welcomed. As a result, strong local companies may use political influence to deter or punish foreign investors.

e. *Changes in Economic Conditions*

Changes in economic conditions in the local or international economy are likely to pose political disturbances for a foreign investor in a host country. These changes create high political risk. As economic conditions change, investors may find persistent trade deficits, non- payment of debts and interest, severe income distribution inequality and deteriorating living standards in a host country.

9.4 Mitigating Political Risks

Diversification of Portfolio investment to multiple countries

In order to reduce or mitigate political risks, investors may choose to diversify their investment by investing in more than one country. This means they shouldn't put their investments in one basket. Investing in more than one country will reduce the level of risk since some countries are higher risk than the others. Investors should also consider diversifying the types of projects they implement. Investing money in positive related projects poses more risks that investing in projets which have negative relationsjhip or which have no any relationship.

Joint Venture with companies in host countries

Multi-national corporations have used this strategy to mitigate political risks. Joint ventures with host country companies may reduce negative government pressure on multi-national companies as governments believe that the companies are contributing to the Gross Domestic Product (GDP) of their nation. In some cases, MNCs have appointed locals with high political influence to be directors of their joint venture.

Political Risk Insurance

Multi-national corporations have the opportunity to insure their foreign investment with the MIGA (Multi-national Investment Guarantee Agency) to cover investment losses due to host government decisions. There are now several more insurance companies that offer political risk insurance. In Kenya, African Trade Insurance Corporation company offers insurance to protect foreign investors against losses as a result of political havoc.

Financing by using local debts

Another interesting way of mitigating political risks is through financing by using host-country debt. A multi-national company, instead of borrowing funds from a foreign country, instead decides to obtain a loan from the bank of the host country where its investments are. In this case, host country governments may hesitate to create problems for MNCs as this may jeopardize the investor's return of borrowed funds.

9.5   Assessment of country risks

In Africa, and truly, around the world, political risks will differ between countries. Some countries are considered more risky than other due to certain conditions or factors existing in the country at the time. Of course those factors may change over time. Foreign investors should access and utilize political risk index indicators developed by international organizations before embarking on the decision to invest in any African country.

One of the indicators of political risks that will vary by country is the political and government system of a country. Some African countries are characterized by numerous political parties which pose the risk of war due to power struggles to lead the government. Examples of this can be seen in those countries where violence breaks out and sometimes develops into war because of acceptance of election results.

Another risk indicator is the frequent changes in government. When government change frequently, investors are put at high risk especially when new governments do not honour agreements and contracts signed by previous governments. International organizations have ranked countries with high government turnover as having high level of political risks because so many foreign investors have suffered great losses during government turnovers.

Inconsistent government policies are also reason for concern and are another indicator of high political risk. When government policies change frequently, this can jeopardize the interest of foreign investors. Policies on profit repatriation, employment and technology transfer, and other policies that affect international business need to be consistent for investors to feel their investment is safe.

Similarly, countries which stay isolated from the international community and global market tend to carry high political risk. Their isolation may be due to the fact that they are not fully integrated into world systems and they, therefore, follow their own political system which may differ greatly from political systems that foreign investors are accustomed to. In Africa, countries like Libya create and follow their own rules and regulations. If a country is not a member in any of international organizations such as World Trade Organization (WTO), World Bank (WB), International Monetary Fund (IMF) and other reputable international organization, investors should be wary of high political risk. Membership in an international organization reduces risk to investors because of conventions that require countries to follow fair-play rules in business. For example, when nationalizing investors' properties, governments in international organizations may be required to compensate the foreign investment while isolated countries may nationalize without compensation.

There are many international organizations with different indicators of political risk which provide guidance to investors who would like to invest in a foreign country. The above discussed indicators are not all-inclusive since there are many models with different indicators already developed and yet to be developed but these points should give interested foreign investors some areas to consider to reduce the risk of their investment.

9.6   Conclusion

The world we live in today is like a small village where businessess and individuals are easily connected . Companies are now not restricted to operate only in only their country of origin. Companies are now venturing into business their beyond their country borders . As the result, they face different challenges in host countries, one of them being the political risks. This chapter defines political risks, the causes of political risks and the categories of political risks. The chapter also highlights different methods on how political risks can be mitigated by companies that opt to do their business beyond their country borders.

Practice Questions

Question 1

What are possible causes of political risk in your country?

Question 2

After viewing your country profile, discuss how political risks influence the operation of your business.

Question 3

Discuss how multi-national corporations in your country survive and thrive despite of existance of political risks.

CHAPTER 10

MANAGING THE BUDGET FUNCTION

10.1   Introduction

The concept of budgeting is widely-used in almost all for-profit and non-profit organizations and is seen as a critical tool for managing financial affairs of the organization. No organization can survive long-term without a clear budgeting strategy.

One major problem which organizations face in budgeting is how they approach the budgeting process. Some companies face serious difficulties as they start implementing their budget when they haven't given critical issues priority before embarking on the figures reflection. Companies should consider these issues before quantifying their budget:

- Define company goals
- Define company objectives (these are more specific than goals as they should include specific dates for expected achievement)
- Identify the programs or activities to be conducted during the budget period
- Use a participatory approach to budgeting
- Quantify the financial implications of the desired programs

Ignoring these important aspects of budgeting will result in poor budgets which may then lead to poor financial performance of the organization. A survey conducted by the author about budgeting found that struggle with budget implementation when the above issues were not carefully considered by managers and instead management rushed into calculating the budget figures.

10.2 Defining Company Goals

Company goals are broad goals which the company desires to achieve over the budget period. These goals should reflect the mission statement of the organization.

Let's take an example of a health provider institution like a hospital.

The broad goal could be:

- Improving quality patient care, and
- Ensuring patient satisfaction.

Another example could be taken from a business organization such as a telecommunication company. The broad goal might be:

- Improving quality customer care, and
- Ensuring customer satisfaction.

10.3 Defining company objectives

Objectives are more specific goals which an organization desires to achieve within a specified period of time. Specific dates should be tied to company objectives.

The specific objectives for the hospital could be:

- Reduce patient complaints by 90%
- Build the capacity of hospital staff
- Improvement of infrastructure (purchase and utilize modern laboratory equipment)

The specific objectives for the Telecommunication Company could be

- Reduce customer complaints by 60%
- Build the capacity of technical staff
- Improvement of infrastructure (purchase and utilize analogy system)

10.4   Identification of company programs or activities

Once the company has identified specific objectives which they want to achieve, it is also important to identify what activities the company will do in order to achieve these objectives. The company programs provide the basis for formulating an effective budget. Ignoring this important step, managers will be working in darkness as far as the budget is concerned.

There have been cases in African companies where managers have just created figures in their budgets without taking into consideration the specific organizational activities and programs. In some cases there have been important programmes left incomplete as donors were unable to provide additional funding for programs left out of the budget. Managers should take this step seriously and understand how critical it is in the creation of an accurate budget.

Using our hospital example again, hospital activities may include:

- Patient counseling programs
- Training of nurses
- Employment of more staff
- Buy Centfridge equipment
- Short courses for staff
- Acquisition of modern equipment

For our telecommunication company, these programs may be run in order to achieve its specific objectives:

- Establish customer complaints handling department
- Training technical staff
- Aquisition and use of modern analogy communication system

10.5   Participation approach to budgeting

These days budgeting cannot and should not be done by a single individual. There are times when managers are tempted to take the responsibility of preparing the whole budget independently instead of involving of other heads of department and staff and engaging in the full budget preparation process. A budget prepared this way can look good at first but there is high possibility of failure during implementation which could affect the company's performance. It is professional and prudent for managers to promote a participatory approach to budgeting where managers and staff participate in all steps of the process through giving input related to their departments. Heads of departments may also discuss budget line items with subordinates to avoid under- or over- budgeting. Cases of omission of line items are greatly reduced when a participatory approach is used.

The participatory approach also motivates employees as they feel that they are valued and are important to the organization. Their behavior towards spending may be more professional and considerate when they are involved in budget formation from the start. Employees will monitor their spending more carefully when they know exactly what is supposed to be spent.

10.6   Budget Preparation

Preparation of the budget is another stage in the budgeting process. A budget can be defined as the quantitative plan of company programs. It can also be defined as a financial reflection of company activities or programs. Once the programs have been approved by the appropriate unit in the organization, it is good to quantify their financial implication to the company. It would be unwise to rush to this stage or to even attempt this stage if previous stages were not completed properly.

Importance of budgeting to the organization

- Budgets create and motivate plans
- Budgets facilitate communication
- Budgets assist in coordination between departments
- Budgets assist in evaluating performance

- Budgets are useful for control purposes
- Budgets can be useful device for influencing employee behaviour

10.7   Problems experienced in the Budgeting Process

The budgeting process is not simple and is rarely accomplished without any challenges or problems. Understanding of the challenges in the budgeting process is important to managers as this understanding will allow them to prepare issues beore they arise. The following are some of the problems which are common in the budget process:

> *Budgets may be interpreted as management pressure:* This view can lead to poor labour relations and the manipulation of accounting records. Many departmental managers consider budgeting to be accountancy work and not relevant to them. However, it is impossible for an accountant in a large organization to understand the unique needs of each department without involving department heads. Some heads of departments resist involvement in budgeting when asked by the accounting team.

> *Departmental conflicts over resource allocation:* It is not possible during the budget process to allocate equal amounts of money to all departments. Some departments, especially core business departments, will have a larger share of the budget as compared to supporting services departments. Because of this, department heads may feel they have been treated unfairly and so conflicts may arise between departments. To prevent these conflicts, transparency and justification of the allocations during the budget process may help.

> *Dysfunctional decision-making for personal gain:* Managers may try to improve their short-run performance at the expense of the organization as a whole. These actions may occur because of managers' ignorance or could happen unintentionally but nonetheless, the negative consequences to the organization remain. An example of this would be when a manager approves certain expenses or denies others to try to show they are saving money while sacrificing important activities.

> ➤ *Managers may build 'slack" into their budgets:* This means that managers understate revenue and overstate costs. When budget ceilings are set and allocations given are less than requested, managers inflate their budgets so that when the budgets are cut, their projects are not as affected.

> ➤ *Incremental budgeting that perpetuates past inefficiencies:* The practice of using incremental budgeting has a tendency of perpetuating past inefficiencies into the coming year. Some of the budget expenditures incurred in past years may not be required in the current year. The practice of simply adding a percentage onto last year's budget is not advised in this case as each year's situation is different from the last. Its important to consider each year separately from the past.

10.8   Uncertainties in budgeting

One thing to remember during the budget planning process is that while you are planning in the present, the budget implementation will take place in the future. The future always is uncertain and therefore, we must try to think of things that might happen in the future. Some considerations may be:

- Change in inflation rates
- Changes in world economic conditions because of wars, gas price inflation, etc.
- Political changes may have adverse effects on the nation economies so business budgets may also be impacted
- Changes in customer demand
- Fluctuations of foreign exchange rates
- Fluctuations of interest rates
- Competitor actions can create a multiplier effect on company budgets
- Donor withdrawals or reductions in funding

10.9   Managing Budget Uncertainties

Management should have contingency plans or should budget for manageable uncertainties. Three methods for this are as follows:

- Use of three budget approaches is recommended. Through this approach, you create your most likely, best possible budget and worst possible budget.
- Use of sensitivity analysis where different variables in the budget are likely to change and the impact to the whole budget can be assessed.
- Use of probabilities- where probalities are attached to different outcomes and then expected values can be easily determined.

10.10   Budget-timing and budget administration

The normal time covered by a budget is one year except for strategic budgets which cover longer than one year. The annual budget can later be broken down into months so that expenses can be tracked at the end of each month. The period of one year is long enough for the organization to easily track its performance in terms of revenue and its expenditures.

It is important, too, for managers to understand that budget need not to be created by a single person but rather by a budget committeeing which is comprised of representatives from all departments contributing either ideas and knowledge. This approach is good as it brings consensus ownership of the budget as heads of departments are involved in the process from start to finish. The heads of departments know exactly what activities are likely to be carried out and the timing of these activities. In order to have an effective budget, heads of departments/sections should involve other members of the department so activities and expenses are not forgotten. One of the main problems in African businesses and organizations is that managers go at the budget for the entire organization alone. When this strategy is used, problems should be expected during the implementation stage.

10.11   Consolidation of departmental Budgets by the Budget Officer

Departmental budgets must be consolidated to create a budget for the whole organization. The accountant has the responsibility of consolidating the departmental budgets into the organizational budget. This means that heads of departments must cooperate with the accountant to facilitate the exercise. The Board of Directors should look over the totality of the whole organizational budget rather than departmental budgets. This does not mean that the board is not interested with departmental budgets, but instead needs a broad understanding of the organization as a whole.

10.12   Types of Budgets

The nature of the business or organization will determine the types of budgets which will be prepared. In manufacturing industries, budgeting might require several types of budgets. In non-manufacturing organizations, requirements may be minimal. Typical examples of budgets required in manufacturing organizations might include production budgets, raw materials purchasing budgets, direct labor budget, sales budget and many others. The job of creating numerous budgets may feel tedious but each of the required` budgets is critical to the financial success of the company. This book does not endeavor to hash out the detailed procedures to prepare all those types of budgets but rather hopes to inform manufactoring managers about the types of budgets they should consider writing in collaboration with accountants who are trained in this type of work.

Non-manufacturing firms generally group their budgets into two main categories: operating and capital budgets. The operating budget should include revenues and expesnes for operational activities while capital expenditure budgets might include sources of income for expected capital expenditures.

10.13   Performance Budgeting

Performance budgeting is a new approach to budgeting systems which differs from traditional budgeting which uses line item budgeting for controlling expenses. Traditional budgeting puts the emphasis on ensuring that money is spent only for the approved purpose without indicating what has actually been accomplished with the money. Traditional budgeting techniques perpetuate past weaknesses and can result in the continuation of activities which are not economically lucrative. With line item budgets, organizations invite micromanagement through creating questions about why activities are being conducted that are not good value for money. The move from traditional method of budgeting to performance budgeting has been made by many public institutions and governement institutions simply because it is seen as a tool to promote accountability, efficiency and helps achieve good results in comparison to the applied resources.

Performance budgeting was developed from the foundation of other budgeting techniques. These techniques include: Zero-based budgeting (ZBB), Management by Objectives (MBO), and the Planning Programming Budget System (PPBS) These techniques were initially utilized by the United States of America government in 1960 (PPBS) and 1970(ZBB). The emphasis of these techniques was on program analysis, multi-year planning, rolling multi-year budgets (PPBS), the evaluation of all programs each year and avoidance of incremental budgeting (ZBB).

There is no standard definition of performance budgeting. However, in every definition, key words are found and so a pieced together definition would be: a system of budgeting that allows managers flexibility to plan and budget the reources required to achieve certain results. The emphasis of performance budgeting is on the relationship between resources/money budgeted and expected results. A positive correlation between the use of resources and results should be clear when this method is implemented correctly.

10.14   Key components of performance budgeting

The following are the key components of performance budgeting:

1. **Flexible:** Performance budgeting is more flexible than traditional budgeting because managers are given flexibility to use resources to achieve desired results rather than being restricted to budget line allotments. In performance budgeting, a lump sum of money is set as the total budget and can be manipulated to meet the

needs of the organization without intense request and approval procedures.

Example:

Most USAID projects allow a buffer that allows 10% of budget to be used in flexible spending without seeking higher level approval.

2. **Inclusive and participatory:** Performance budgeting is more inclusive than traditional budgeting because policy makers, managers and citizens are all part of the budget discussion from strategic planning to identification of spending priorities, setting performance indicators and monitoring performance. This inclusivity complies with the concept of citizen engagement in public budgeting.

3. **Long-term perspective:** Performance budgeting has a long-term perspective as it links strategic objectives and money allocation over the life of the project. The focus is on how the resource allocation in the budget period helps achieve long-term strategic objectives.

10.15   Conclusion

Budgeting is a very wider subject that one chapter cannot exhaust all matters related to the topic. However, this chapter has discussed briefly most common issues that can help chief Excutive officers and Managers to understand proper budgeting of business activities for bettter performances of their organization.

The chapter has explained the three key budgeting process and gave the simple definition of budgeting. The chapter has also discussed the importance of participatory budgeting, problems experienced in the budget process as well as the uncertainities that can impair the implementation of the budget. Furthermore the chapter explain the different types of budgets and discussed more on the key componets of performance budgeting.

Practice Questions

Question 1

The time for preparation of the annual budget and its forwarding to the Board of Directors has come. Before preparing the budget, you are required to come up with goals, objectives and programs as the basis for preparation of your budget.

Required

Prepare the goals, objectives and programs for year 2020 .
What do you think are the limitations for your programs?
Prepare the annual budget for year 2020.

Question 2

Masanja is a Chief Executive Officer of Maweleni Hospital. He has approached you, as his friend, to help him to prepare a budget for the anti-malaria project he expects to submit to World Vision, International to secure the funding of the project. The following are the programs which the project is expected to perform in the year 2006:

- Malaria sensitization program to villagers which will costs $2,000,000/=. The facilitator of the program will be paid $50 for each of the 5 days of the program.
- Mosquito nets worth $10,000 will be distributed to 5000 families in the neighboring villages surrounding the village
- Purchase of a Land cruiser worth $34,000 to use during program activities
- Salaries to field personnel will total $25,000,000
- Clinical equipment worth $6,000 will be purchased for accurate malaria diagnosing
- Field consummables required including malaria treatment medications Duo-cotexin at $ 10,780 and SPM at $7,970)
- Staff training at KCMC Hospital will cost $1,200

- Provision of lunch to motivate staff working long hours on the project $350 per month
- Laboratory renovations for effective malaria testing which will require $20,000

    Collaboration with other institutions to ensure quality blood sample testing. The sample testing will also be done at the National Medical Research Institute at a cost of $5,679

Required

Prepare the Budget for Maweleni Hospital for the Year 2019

Question 3

You have recently been appointed as the CEO of a newly constructed hospital in Mlanje responsible for overseeing personnel and financial matters of the hospital by the Board of Mlanje Hospital. It is now time to prepare the budget for the next financial year, 2020. It is not your responsibility to calculate budget numbers but you are required to work with your subordinates to come up with a budget and submit it for board approval.

The following matters should be taken into consideration when preparing your budget:

- Number of inpatients is expected to increase to 20,000 people in the next year while outpatient number will be 40,000 people. Inpatient fees ares $50 per person and outpatient fee are $30 per person.
- Your hospital has been designated by Ministry of Health (MOH) to receive a grant of $30,000 in the year 2019. The Australian government will also support your hospital with $50,000 (USD).
- Total salaries for all medical personnel total $200,000 per year
- In order to address problems with x-rays, the hospital will buy a new x-ray machine for $16,000 from Japan. The importation costs will incur an additional $2,000 in tax
- In order to improve quality of patient care services, two nurses will attend a short-course training in Kampala, Uganda. The cost of

the training will be $3,500 for the two nurses and they will require a per-diem of $450 each for 14 days.

- The following medical supplies will be procured from different suppliers

    1. Syringes @ $1,340
    2. Cotton wool @ $790
    3. Disinfectants @ $1,800

    - The present laboratory will require consummables costing $1,000.

Required

Based on this information, prepare a preliminary budget for 2019 for approval by the Board.

Question 4

Experts point out that one of the most important tasks of management accounting is the regular monitoring of cash flow funds coming into the company each month minus funds going out.

Required

Comment on the above statement and include the benefits gained from preparation of cash budgets by organizations in your response.

Question 5

Despite the benefits of budgeting systems, being a major feature of most control systems, there are problems which may arise from the way in which the budget processes are implemented.

Required

List and explain any five problems that are associated with the budget development process.

Question 6

For developing countries like Kenya, the budgeting process is uncertain in that it takes place in a volatile and sometimes unpredictable environment. Uncertainties include high inflation, frequent changes in exchange rates, consumer demand changes and other related factors.

Required

Explain any three methods that could be applied to cope with these uncertainties

Question 7

Discuss the concept of performance budgeting and explain how it could be applied in your organization.

Question 8

How does performance budgeting differ from traditional budgeting?

Question 9

What are challenges are likely in preparing and implementing performance budgeting in your organization?

CHAPTER 11

MANAGEMENT OF CASH

11.1 Introduction

All business organizations requires cash in order to meet their day to day business activity needs. Inadequate cash on hand may lead poor business performance. Many problems are caused by inadequate knowledge on how cash should be managed. There are two major cash problems which a business may experience: excessive cash or inadequate cash problems. Both can create problems for the organization.

11.2 Motives for Holding Cash

A company or an organization need not keep cash on hand just for the sake of having it. When this is done, the opportunity to generate additional income or profit is jeopardized because cash could have been invested somewhere to grow rather than sitting without gain. However, having inadequate cash on hand can also create problems for the organization. Cash must be managed prudently at all times and cash should only be kept for specific reasons. The following reasons are some of the only justifiable reasons for keeping cash:

a. **Transaction Motives**: This refers to keeping cash for meeting day to day business operating costs. The availability of cash for such purposes will help the organization to conduct its business without delays in making payments for purchases, wages, salaries, taxes and other operating costs.

b. **Precautionary Motives:** Meaning that cash is being held so that the organization is prepared for any emergency or contingency that requires immediate cash availability. It is important to note, though, that this does not mean that the organization should store a lot of cash in the office as this is not safe. A safe approach to holding money with precautionary motives is to invest the money in assets that can be easily converted to cash when needed. Money for these precaution purposes may be invested in market securities or shares.

c. **Speculative Motives:** Opportunities to make profit arise in the business world often and without notice. Only those businesses with cash resources can tap into these opportunities and so it is important for business organizations to hold cash in case these opportunities arise. The speculative motive helps management stay abreast of opportunities such as falling share prices and currency revaluation to make more money for their business organization.

11.3   Cash Planning

In order to avoid problems related to inadequate cash availability in organizations, management needs to plan for its cash. The planning of cash is necessary for the following reasons:

a. To avoid problems associated in the lack of cash to pay debts and other maturing cash obligations. Lack of cash can lead to possibility of insolvency or other problems such as employee strikes when salary payments are late or incomplete.

b. To ensure adequate cash is available at all times for day to day business transactions.

c. To arrange financing in a period of cash shortage. Where there is proper planning of cash management, companies can predict likely shortage periods and and negotiate for an overdraft from the bank, if needed.

d. To provide information for decision-making related to cash surpluses. The use of surplus cash should be carefully planned for so that cash is not wasted with little or no benefit to the organization.

e. To accurately estimate the remaining cash balance at the end of each month.

f. To increase management awareness of potential cash shortages & surpluses.

11.4 Cash Management

Effective cash management requires the following three issues be addressed properly so that the right amount of cash is available at the right time. Good cash management requires:

1. **Accurate Cash flow forecasting & monitoring**

    Forecasting will involve the assessing likely sources of cash inflow as well as cash flow over a certain time period. Forecasting also requires monitoring the forecasted cash flow. Accurate forecasts are based on the nature of the business, the business environment, and business trends observed from past company cash performance. The projection of future cash flow is easier when there is a budget and can be substantiated with business expenditure patterns from the past period, inflation rate changes, exchange rate fluctuations as well as other conditions that are likely to prevail.

2. **Short-term borrowing when needed**

    In cases where the company is experiencing a cash shortage, management should be in position to acquire additional cash through short-term borrowing. This is not easy if management is unaware of available opportunities in their business field or is unsure of how to go about actually securing the needed funds. Short-term borrowing can take place through overdraft facilities at banks the business uses regularly. Of course business managers must remember that even overdrafts have costs as they will be paid back with interest.

3. **Investing any surplus cash**

When managers fail to invest surplus company cash, this indicates poor cash management. Managers should stay abreast of investments that surpluses can be placed in so that opportunities further increase profits are not missed. Surplus cash can be invested in government treasury bills and bonds, fixed assets, and other marketable securities. We will discuss surplus cash handling further a bit later but at this point, managers should be aware of the need to invest surplus cash.

11.5   Major Causes of cash shortages

The factors explained below are likely to be major causes of cash shortages at the organizational level. In trying to identify the causes of cash shortage at company level, managers should understand that not all factors apply to every company. Some factors may cause cash shortages in one company and have no impact on another company. Let us look into a few of these causes:

a. **Customers not paying their debts:** In this scenario, a company may sell its goods on credit but find that debts remain unpaid over a long period of time. This problem may be created because of poor credit policies, poor recording of debts and lack of strong debt collections procedures.

b. **Refusal to sell on credit:** In the competitive world of business, there are some businesses which simply cannot stay in business without offering sales on credit. When competitors sell on credit, refusal of your company to do so can jeopardize your company's cash flow.

c. **Disruption to production:** In manufacturing settings, production can be disrupted for any number of reasons including electricity cuts, strikes, or lack of needed production resources. These disruptions will likely affect sales and hence lead to cash shortages.

d. **Business failure:** When a business is unable to sell enough of its products, the business will obviously experience cash flow shortages. Business failure can be caused by new competitors in the market, better substitute products, etc.

e. **Over investment in fixed assets:** When a company uses its cash resources to invest in fixed assets which do not actively generate additional cash, the company may experience a cash shortage. Therefore, investments in fixed assets need to be carefully planned to avoid cash flow problems.

f. **Over trading, rapid expansion,and/or insufficient working capital:** In periods of rapid expansion, large amounts of cash are needed to launch a new product, opening another branch, etc. These sudden large expenses often lead to cash shortages in the short-term.

g. **Poor credit control**: Poor credit control is often caused by loose credit control policies, lack of staff skilled in credit management, poor accounting systems, mismanagement and corruption and can result in shortage of cash.

h. **Excessive credit:** Due to lack of proper credit policy or a loose credit policy, a company may give out excessive credits which are uncollectible and hence result in a shortage of cash.

11.6   Solutions to company cash shortages

The above discussed problems are not inclusive and so your company may experience other problems leading to cash shortages. Management needs to carefully diagnose the causes of cash shortages before embarking on any remedies. The following are recommended solutions to address company cash shortages:

1. **Sell idle fixed assets:** Management should identify idle assets and dispose of them at market prices to improve its cash inflow. Board approval is required in this case to avoid selling company assets at throw away prices .

2. **Sell and lease back assets:** Most of the time, the acquisition of fixed assets will require a company to have a substantial lump sum

of cash available. When a company is experiencing a cash shortage, it may be cheaper for the company to sell some fixed assets and start leasing them back. In this scenario cash can be increased with immediacy and the company can continue using the fixed assets without owning them.

3. **Stimulate sales through price discounts:** This technique can be used to encourage more customers to buy and to pay promptly which in turn, improve cash inflow. Terms of credit must clearly specify what percentage of discount will be given for customers who pay within set time periods (i.e. 15, 30 or 60 days).

4. **Improve debtor control and chase debts:** In order to improve cash collection, companies may need to improve their debt collection mechanisms. This can be achieved by sending reminder letters, telephone calls or e-mails. In some more challenging cases, other methods can be used such as involving court brokers or taking legal actions. The company should not resort quickly to legal action for debt collection, though, because this can tarnish a company's reputation and may end up in greater financial loss if the case is lost or lengthy. Arbitration is advisable as a first step in dealing with hard to recoup losses.

5. **Proper Financial Recording Systems:** Improving debt collection also requires the company to improve its financial recording systems. The use of computerized accounting systems is highly advisable when company transactions are large in number or amount. Good accounting packages are readily available and efficient in tracking debtors.

6. **Tighten credit control:** Where there is no credit policy or there is a loose credit policy, there will be cash inflow problems. Tightening credit control is likely to reduce the rate of debt defaulters, help avoid theft and prevent other malpractice.

7. **Raise more capital:** The company can raise more capital by issuing more shares to the public if it is a listed company or through borrowing money from cheaper sources.

8. **Arrange overdraft facilities:** In some countries overdraft fees are so high that taking a short-term overdraft is not advisable. However, the use of bank overdrafts can be very useful in helping

to solve short-term cash shortages. Obtaining bank overdrafts should not be difficult when a company has a good relationship with the bank where an overdraft is sought.

11.7   Other ways of improving cash flow

Cash flow problems can also be reduced by looking on the side of cash outflow. When cash outflows are managed, the company is likely to have cash for financing its business activities. The following techniques can be used to reduce cash outflows:

- Lengthen suppliers' credit terms by negotiating a rescheduling of debt payments
- Postpone investments; some investments can be briefly delayed to reduce cash problems
- Reduce stock-holding: Adopt a 'Just in Time' production technique (JIT) which means stocking only a few specific items which difficult to obtain and purchase all other stock only when needed. Know the availability of items in the market before using this technique. Purchase stock on credit. Sometimes it is wise to purchase goods on credit and pay later and use the available cash to meet the immediate costs of the company
- Ask trade creditors for extended credit. In this case management can negotiate with trade creditors to extend the payment period . This can help management to have adequate cash to pay other immediate bills.
- Improve planning, monitoring and control.- Management team should seat down and plan their cashflow rather than spending cash haphazardly . They should also monitor and control their cash movement in order to minimize cash leakages to unplanned activities.

11.8   Introduction to cash budgeting

One of the best ways that an organization can manage its cash is to prepare a cash budget. The cash budget will serve as a benchmark for monitoring cash inflow and outflow over a set period of time. Normally cash budgets are prepared on a weekly or monthly basis so that excess cash or cash shortages are expected and understood. Cash budgets also help managers keep up with the cash balance at the end of the specified period.

It is the responsibility of management during cash shortage periods to find ways to mitigate the problem before the company becomes unable to cover day to day operation costs and faces financial problems. Forecasted cash shortages can be solved using any of the ways outlined above and when there is excess cash, short-term investments can be thought through by management.

Components of Cash Budgets

The following are the major components of the cash budget:

Cash inflow sources

All sources of cash inflow have to be included in the preparation of a cash budget. Cash inflow can come from different sources such as:

1. **Cash sales** when the company sells goods on cash basis.
2. **Collection from credit sales** when the company sells goods on credit and payment collection is made at an agreed upon time after the sale.
3. **Sale of fixed assets**
4. **Loans from fund lenders**
5. **Interest from bank deposits**
6. **Grants from donors**

This list of cash inflow sources is not all-inclusive. Management of a company should be able to predict other funding sources available during any targeted budget planning period.

Cash outflow sources

All areas of expenditure where actual cash leaves the organization must be recorded. Cash outflow sources will include payment for normal operating costs as well as expenditures paid for capital items such as the procurement of machines and vehicles.

Net Cash Flows

This is the difference between the total cash inflow and total cash outflow which is used when the cash budget is being prepared.

Opening Cash Balance

This is the balance of cash on hand at the beginning of the planning period.

Closing Cash Balance

This is the figure arrived at after the opening cash balance is added to the net cash flow. This will be an opening cash balance in the beginning of the next planning period. If closing balance at the end of month of January was $1,000, for example, then the opening cash balance at the beginning of February will also be $1,000.

Minimum desired cash balance

Normally the management sets a minimum balance of cash the company should maintain at all times. The determined amount depends on the company's needs as well as its capacity to generate future cash flow. Once the minimum balance has been set and monitored, a comparison with the cash closing balance should be conducted to determine whether the company has excess cash which needs to be invested or if the company has a shortage of cash and therefore needs to borrow.

Transactions which do not involve cash movement should not appear in any of the above categories. The primary purpose of preparing a cash budget is to track actual inflow and outflow of cash. Items such as depreciation charges, profits on disposal of fixed assets, provisions for expenditures and reserves do not involve the movement of cash and so they are not relevant to this documentation.

11.9 Procedures for the preparation of a cash budget

The preparation of a cash budget is not difficult when it is done following the recommended steps below.

1. Determine the cash budget period required
2. Determine all cash inflow sources
3. Deduct the cash outflow sources from the cash inflow sources
4. Note the difference as the Net Cash Flow
5. Add the opening balance to the Net Cash flow to arrive at the closing cash balance
6. Deduct the minimum balance required from the closing cash balance

When these steps are followed, the end result will be either surplus cash which should be invested or a cash deficit which will require finding short-term finance options to close the deficit.

11.10 Format of a cash budget

The following format for cash budgeting is simple and can be adopted easily by anyone attempting to start or update a cash budgeting system. If your cash budget is for more than one period, columns and rows may be added to the table.

XYB COMPANY LIMITED
CASH BUDGET FOR THE MONTH OF JAN 2007

		Amount
A	Cash Inflow	XXXX
B	Cash Outflow	(XXXX)

C Net Cash Flows (A-B)   XXXX

D Opening Balance   <u>XXXX</u>

E Closing Balance (C+D)   XXXX

F Minimum Balance   <u>XXXX</u>

G SURPLUS/ (SHORTAGE)/ (E-F)   XXX/ (XXX)

11.11   Timing of cash inflow

In preparing the cash budget, it is also important to understand that cash inflows and outflows will have different timings which may impact cash balances at certain times. In case of inflow sources, especially when sales are made on credit, the actual cash collection from the debtor may take a significant amount of time. Get a clear understanding of the credit terms from the start so that that forecast of cash flow is more accurate. Typical examples of credit collections may include:

1. Sales are made on credit but 70% of credit sales are collected in the month of the sale and 30% will be collected in the following month.
2. Sales are made on credit but 70% of credit sales are collected one month after sales with 25% collected in the following month and 5% uncollectible.
3. Credit sales are collected over a three-month period in the ratio of 60%, 30%, and 9%, with 1% uncollectible
4. All sales are on credit. Half are paid for in the month of sale and half in the following month.

The above arrangements are simply suggestions for credit collections timings but should should give some guidance on how to clarify your collection timings so that forecasts of actual cash inflow can be accurately made.

11.12   Timing of cash outflow

Some companies may also be buying goods on credit from their suppliers and therefore won't pay the entire cost outright but will follow payment structures set by the supplier. In such cases, typical payment patterns should be known and used to make accurate forecasts of cash outflow. The payment patterns can be extended to other services where the company enjoys some services on credit terms while payments are made later.

Illustrating Question

Mama Lele Limited needs a cash budget for the month of September, 2007. The following information is available (all figures are in US dollars):

1. The cash balance on September 1, 2007 is $7,500.
2. Actual sales for July and August and expected sales for September are as follows:

   - Cash sales for July $5,000; Credit sales $25,000
   - Cash sales for August $5,250; Credit sales $30,000
   - Cash sales for September $6,500; Credit sales $35,000

3. Credit sales are collected over a three-month period in a ratio of 60%, 30%, 9%, with one-percent uncountable.
4. Purchase of inventory will total $18,000 for September. Seventy percent of a month's purchases are paid for in the month of purchase.
5. Accounts payable for August purchases total $6,150 which will be paid in September.
6. Selling and administrative expenses are budgeted at $14,000 for September. This amount includes $5,000 for depreciation.
7. Dividends of $5,000 will be paid during September and equipment costing $12,000 will be purchased.
8. The company wishes to maintain a minimum cash balance of $5,000. An open line of credit is available from the company's bank to boost their cash position as needed.

Required

Prepare a cash budget for the month of September. Indicate any borrowing that will be necessary during the month.

Solution:

Mama Lele Ltd Cash Budget for the Month of Sept 2007

		USD
Cash Inflows		
Cash sales	6500	
Credit sales	32250	
Total Inflows		38,750
Less: Cash Outflow		
Purchases (70% of 18,000)	12,600	
Accounts Payable	6,150	
Selling and Adminstative ($14,000-$5000)	9,000	
Dividends	5,000	
Equipments	12,000	
Total : Cash Outflows		44,750
Net cashflows		(6,000)
Add: Opening Cash Balance		7,500
Closing Cash Balance		1,500
Less: Minimum Caash Required Balance		5,000
Deficit		**3,500**

Note

1. Collection based on percentage

9% of July sales (9% x 25,000)	2250
30% of August sales (30% x $ 30,000)	9000
60% of September sales (60% x $ 35,000)	21,000
Total	**32,250**

11.13   Conclusion

The chapter on cash management should help Chief Executive Officers and managers to understand the importance of planning for the company liquidity in order to avoid unneccessary problems associated with lack of cash. The topic has tried to explain the motives for holding cash and why cash planning is important for the organization.

The chapter also explains what really entails cash planning, the causes of cash shortages and gives suggestions on how organizations can deal with cash shortages and it shows simple method of cash budgets. The chapter also highlights on how management can utilize excess surplus cash when it arises.

Practice Questions

Question 1

Discuss the reasons for cash budgeting and its benefits.

Question 2

What are likely consequences of inadequate cash or excess cash at the company level?

Question 3

There will always be times when companies experience cash shortages for a multitude of reasons. Discuss some reasons why a company may experience cash shortages and how you would advise a company to deal with this problem.

Question 4

Mama Tete projected the following profit and loss account (in USD) on a monthly basis.

	October	November	December	January
Sales	80,000	120,000	60,000	80,000
Cost of Sales	60,000	90,000	45,000	60,000
Gross Profits	20,000	30,000	15,000	20,000
Expenses	16,000	18,000	15,000	16,000
Net Profit	**4,000**	**12,000**	**NIL**	**4,000**

The following additional information is available

(a) All sales are on credit. Half are paid for in the month of sale and half in the following month.
(b) Debts in the end month of September amounted to $30,000
(c) All purchases are on credit and are paid in the month after purchase. Creditors at the end of September amounted to $20,000

(d) Stocks at the end of September amounted to $34,000

(e) It is desired to maintain stocks at the end of each month equal to 50% of the next month's sales.

(f) Expenses which include $2,000 per month for depreciation are paid as they arise.

(g) New fixed assets will be purchased in October and paid for in December. They will cost $10,000

(h) The cash balance at the end of September is expected to be $2,000

Required

Draw up a cash budget for each of the three months: October, November and December.

CHAPTER 12

MANAGING TAX AFFAIRS OF THE COMPANY

12.1   Introduction

In modern business organizations, understanding tax laws helps managers recognize their tax obligations, determine what tax incentives are available to them, know what to do when tax disputes arise, and understand how to, for example, design better remuneration packages for their employees. It is also important to appreciate the role of tax consultants in advising management on issues of tax planning for issues such as embarking on a major investment project. . Tax laws of countries are always changing and so managers must constantly re-familiarize themselves with changes that affect their business organizations.

12.2   What is taxation?

Taxation has existed throughout the history of human societies and has always been a part of leadership and governance. Although taxes were not collected in monetary currency as they are today, tax collection existed through relevant exchanges of items of value. During the time when barter trade was common, tax was collected in terms of goods and when gold and silver were deemed valuable, they were used as a means of exchange and were collected from taxpayers.

Looking at the history of kingdoms accross the world, we can see that kings collected goods, silver, gold and other items as head taxes from citizens. Even the bible contains records of various kingdoms such as Solomon's where the Israelites had to pay taxes. Tax collection has never been voluntary and has always been enforced to people..

With this knowledge of taxation, we begin to form varying definitions of taxation. One definition of taxation considers tax as a compulsory contribution to the government by both corporate and non-corporate parties in order to support government provision of public services. Corporate citizens include individuals and corporations and taxes are levied on properties, commodities and transactions which are undertaken by these principal entities for taxation.

Another definition describes taxation as voluntary and compulsory contributions of money by individuals and corporate entities to the government so as to meet public expenditures. This definition of taxation gives a broader meaning by including the word voluntary-- meaning that taxpayers are not forced to pay taxes. Through this definition, it seems that citizens have the option to pay or not to pay tax. In the most literal form, this is true—citizens are free to pay taxes or not, but in reality, taxation is not voluntary when citizens need to consume products. Citizens may only pay taxes when they consume goods and services of which taxes are attached to. The definition makes more sense when individuals spend money on lotteries and other goods of which taxes are levied on as commodities.

12.3 Why taxation is important

The major way governments raise funds to support public expenditures is through taxation. The question that governments need to answer is, what is included in public expenditures? Government expenditures include the provision of social services, maintenance of law and order, ability to defend the country as well as other undertakings which the private sector cannot provide. Countries which cannot raise enough funds through taxation are likely to have difficulties in their balancing payments. Most developing countries, due to an inability to collect enough taxes, have experienced problems funding their operational and development budgets and tend to rely on donors support. A country like Kenya, by 2009, had successully managed to fund its budget at 100% while Tanzania managed to fund its budget only 65% and the rest was donor funds.

Taxation is used by most countries as a policy instrument to protect local industries. When imported goods are levied with high taxes, locally produced products produced are given lower tax rates tax rates which will result in prices of local products being cheaper than imported ones. However, today, with regional intergrations such as the East Africa Community and tax harmonization within the member countries, taxation is used to protect the industries of all member states.

Governments can also use taxation as an instrument of discouraging certain habits which are considered to be harmful to the public such as use of tobacco, cigarettes, and alcohol by imposing high taxes these products. The major question about this type of taxation is: why should governments create laws that prohibit the use of these products if they are harmful to the citizens? The answer to this question is that governments depend on tax revenue from these sources and, at the same time, people should have freedom to make choices about what products they will or will not consume.

Governments also use taxation as an instrument of mobilizing and accumulating capital from the general public and concentrating the capital for capital development projects and investments. Governments cannot spend all their funds in recurring expenditures but part of the funds collected through taxation should be used for development and investments such as construction of infrastructure systems including roads, dams and power generating plants.

Other objective of government taxation include taxing for wealth distribution among the society. This is achieved through taxing rich people more so that services can be provided to the entire public. Taxation of this type is called progressive taxation and occurs when people with high incomes will pay higher taxes than people with lower incomes.

Finally, taxation is used to help the government allocate available in-country resources to bring development to geographical areas which are underdeveloped. Government strategies are used to ensure even distribution of development in a country and more resources through taxation means there will be more funds to support infrastructure development and economic projects.

12.4   Tax classfication

There are various types of tax classification which are useful for understanding tax as used in various tax jurisdictions. Classification of taxes can are done in a number of ways to help policymakers come up with tax systems that are favourable to both governments and taxpayers.

1. **Head Tax:** A tax on the existence of a particular type of taxpayers such as a levy of a certain amount paid by all individuals over minor age. This is not so common in most tax jurisdictions. Countries like Tanzania, Kenya and Uganda, during colonial regimes had head taxes levied on individuals above 18 years.

2. **Income Tax:** This is levied on individual income or corporate income. The income tax on individuals is termed as "Pay as you earn" (P.A.Y.E) although some countries have other taxes levied on individuals. Taxation on corporations is levied on both resident and non-resident companies. Tax rates vary from one jurisdiction to another. Some tax jurisdictions have the same rate of income tax both types of companies while others have different rates depending on the resident status of the company. Income taxes are progressive in nature simply because they are paid depending on the income level of the taxpayer. The higher the income, the higher the taxes and vice versa. In terms of compliance, governments do not experience many challenges in compliance by taxpayers.

3. **Commodity Taxes:** These are taxes levied on commodities. As people consume certain products, they pay taxes knowingly or unknowingly as taxes can be built into the product price. Other types of commodity taxes include value added taxes and sales taxes. Commodity taxes are considered to be regressive taxes where people with less income have more pinch than the ones with higher income.

4. **Wealth Taxes:** These are levied on the wealth of the taxpayer. These include taxes such as estate duties, property taxes and capital gains taxes. Depending on tax administrative efficiency, some countries try and later abandon estate duties. In Africa, Tanzania is one of the countries which does not have estate duties. Tanzania abandoned estate duties because the collection costs against the money gained was not cost efficient.

5. **User Tax:** User taxes differ from one tax jurisdiction to another. They are taxes levied on use of a facility such as toll bridges, fuel or roads. Depending on the cost of administering these taxes, various jursidictions have different ways of charging these taxes to the public.

6. **Tariff:** is a tax or duty usually imposed on imported goods to increase the price of such goods relative to domestic goods.

12.5   The Role of Managers in company tax affairs

In order to ensure that an organization is voluntarily complying with the tax laws in a country where it does business, management of the organization have to ensure that it plays a number of different roles such as the ones which are mentionred below :

a. To ensure that the organization is keeping proper books of accounts that are the basis for prepartion of financial statements. It is through financial statements, tax authorities can determine the corporate taxes.

b. To ensure compliance to all tax laws of the country in which their company are oprerating. Compliance means the company is paying all its tax dues to the tax authorities

c. Ensure that company staff involved in the tax matters of the organization are competent enough to interpret the tax laws. Competency means that staff are capable to understand the tax laws, compute appropriate taxes and pay the taxes at the right time

d. Ensure that staff in the finance deaprtment are able to compute the right tax the company is supposed to pay

e. To ensure that company staff are filing proper tax returns to tax authority

f. To ensure that there is proper relationship with government tax authorities

g. To ensure that the organization is involving tax consultants to help to do tax planning so as to take advatanges of all tax laws loopholes in order to minimize tax liability without breaking the laws of the country.

12.6   Conclusion

Taxation is a broader subject that requires the study of laws that impose tax liability on individual or corporate entity. However, tax laws in any jurisdiction are many and Chief Executive Officers and managers are not expected to know or study all the laws as they are not tax specilaists. Their role is to maintaina general understanding of taxation to help them ensure that the finance personll are implementing their tax responsibilities. This topic has highlighted the importance of taxation and explained the different types of taxation. The topic gives also a brief explanation on what should be the role of Chief Executives and managers in dealing with the taxation affairs of the organization.

Practice Questions

Question 1

Discuss the consquences of non compliance to tax laws for your organization

Question 2

What strategies should management of the organization employ in order to ensure that it complies to its tax obligations ?

Question 3

Discuss how management can maintain proper relationship with the tax authority .

CHAPTER 13

MANAGING OF DEBTORS

13.1   Introduction

In modern business, the selling of goods and services has become an art that if not managed carefully, company sales are likely to be low while competitors could be making good sales. One of the ways of increasing company sales is selling goods on credit with cash collection on a future date.

While company sales are likely to increase due to selling goods on credit, there is also a possibility that company cash flow can be affected if debtors are not paying back their debts. Management needs to understand that inability to collect debts affects company cash flow and profitability which could lead to problems such as an inability to pay daily operational costs and difficulties in managing financial obligations—both of these problems could lead to insolvency if not resolved. There are many examples of companies which failed to collect their debts and now no longer exist.

There are many reasons as to why companies might fail to collect their debts even though they may be doing very well in terms of sales. Here are some of the reasons:

- **Poor Credit Policy:** The policy could be very loose with loopholes for non-payment of debts
- **Shortage of qualified debt collection and recording staff**
- **Poor accounting systems** in which customer accounts/records are not in order

- **Collusion** between company debt collectors and customers
- **Poor customers follow-up mechanisms** to follow debts payment
- **Unclear credit policy**
- **Delays in updating customer accounts**
- **Inability to handle debt defaulters**
- **Poor communication skills among staff** which may anger customers and make debt collection even more unlikely

13.2   The need for a strong credit policy

For all business organizations which deal with customers, especially those who sell their products on both cash and credit bases, it is critical to have effective debt collection policies and proper management of their cash flow. Credit policies are simple guidelines developed by companies to guide how credit can be given to customers and how and when cash collection will occur. The existence of credit policy in a company provides a structured approach to risk management and the debt collection process. It also helps ensure that the credit department focuses on what the company considers vital.

13.3   Advantages of having a credit policy

Credit policies have the following advantages for a company:

➢ Serve as an internal documents that identify all set and agreed upon procedures that govern the organization's credit functions.
➢ Provide guidance to company staff responsible for debt management in their day to day activities.
➢ Give a standard framework to achieve transparency.
➢ Limit bad debts and improve cash flow.
➢ Assure a degree of consistency among departments on how to deal with customers and manage day to day issues related debt collection and credit

13.4   Types of Credit Policies

Basically, there are two types of credit policies which a company can design to enable proper and easy collection of debts from customers. The company can have etheir a too tight credit policy or a loose credit policy. Both of them have benefits and consequences, therefore management has to consider carefully the kind of the credit policy it desires to have.

A too tight credit policy is the one which is detailed enough to cover everthing and leave no room for negotiations or accommodate anything new agreements between the company and its customers. In this case company employees have no option to give new ideas on how business should be conducted.

A too loose credit policy is the one which is not tight, it gives rooms for negotiations and does not give details on how each steps on business has to be conducted. A too loose credit policy might enhance creativity of employees to handle different business situations.

Benefits of tight credit policies

The following are some of the benefits of having a tight credit policies.

a. Cash flow improvements – Tight credit policy might help to squeeze customers to pay their dues on time and hence improve cashflows
b. It is makes easier to forecast the future cashflows of cash collection
c. It can help to reduce bad debts as you are likely to increase cash collections from debtors
d. It can help to reduce the costs of debt collection
e. When cashflows is improved as more money is collected from customer, it can lead to improved company stability.

Consequences of Tight Credit Policies

Tight credit policies may pose a lot of consequences to the organization. However, if managed well the consequnces can be minimized and the organization can benefit more from such policies. The following are some of the consequences of a tight credit policy:

a. Risk of losing existing and potential customers- When the policy is too tight existing customers may be discontented and decide to leave to other competitors who are doing the same business. The departure of exsiting customers sends a signal to ponteal customers who might decline buying products or services from your company.

b. Difficulty in finding new and potential customers- When the credit policy is too tight it may disourage new customers to join the company especially when the credit policies of competitors is loose.

c. Loss of market shares- When customers leave the company it means that your market share might also decline

d. Loss of company competitive advantage

e. Risk of losing long-term customers- Long term customers might opt to deal with new companies

f. Hampers company growth- There is high possibility of sales reduction. When sales declines due to customers leaving the company growth can be affected.

Benefits of loose credit policy

There are few benefits that are assossiated with a loose credit policy. A loose credit might attract more customers to like your company, as the result you are likely to increase the sales, increased profitability and hence increase the market share and improve your cash flows only if you have good plan to collect cash from customers.

Consequences of very loose credit policy

Despite the benefits of a loose credit policy there are number of consquences of such policy. The following consequences are likely to impact the organization

a. **Liquidity problems: S**ince the policy is too loose the company might not be able to follow up the payment of credit by customers and hence create shortages .

b. **High rate of defaulting customers**: Simply because they will be no one seriously following the payment of credit it is easy for customers to deafult the full amount of money owed.

c. **Increased bad debts:** Follwing high rate of defaulting customers the there could be high rate of increased debts which undermines the profitability of the company.

d. **Poor cashflow can lead to other challenges to the organization such as inability to meet its financial obligations such as paying the creditors, which can lead to insolvency problems.**

13.5   Variables to credit policy

Any credit policy designed should address the problems which cause the organization to improve its cash flow collections. In designing the credit policy a number of variables must be included in the policy. However, these variables depend on the business itself, its customers and business environment it operates in. Examples of variables include:

➢ **Credit Standards:** These are criteria for selecting customers who should be given credit.

➢ **Credit Terms of Sales:** Including such issues as credit period, cash discounts to be given, collection procedures, and general policies and procedures related to credit

➢ **Credit Evaluation:** The system used to evaluate credit

➢ **Credit Responsibility:** A determination at the company level who should have the responsibility to handle credits

13.6   Improving debt collection at the company level

Any sales efforts by the company which are not followed by effective collection or recovery of debt are likely to jeopardize their cash inflow and lead to challenges. The following suggestions, if taken into consideration, will improve a company's debt collection effectiveness:

- *Streamline accounting and recording function of debts:* Customer accounts need be in order and updated on timely basis. Use of computerized accounting systems is highly recommended in the modern business environment.
- *Create and maintain a clear credit policy with clearly defined clauses:* Avoid using a very loose or very tight credit policy which may result in have negative impacts on debt collection efforts.
- *Ensure adequate and trained staff are available to make follow-up on debts.*
- *Use proper reminder letters* that motivate customers to pay their debts
- *Give discounts to customers who pay on time.*
- *Use court-brokers for frequent debt defaulters.* However, other efforts should be used first though to prevent a negative company reputation
- *Recognize that there are cases where customers should be taken to court.* Court cases are important especially if the amount involved is extreme, the customer is uncooperative and and all efforts of collecting the payments have failed.

In countries where debt factoring companies exist, the company may opt to use debt factoring but other factors need be considered before choosing this option.

13.7 Debt Factoring

Debt factoring is a new phenomenon in the African setting and for African companies. Only in a very few countries where financial policies are liberalized do we see debt factoring institutions popping up. Even if these aren't present now, they will be in the near future as the world is a small global village.

Debt factoring is defined a system in which company debts are sold at discount price on a cash basis to a financial institution (the factoring company). These situatinos occur when a company sells its goods or services on credit terms to different customers and the future collection is expected. Debt factoring has many advantages to a company which sells its debts.

Here are a few examples of the advantages of debt factoring:

a. The Company that sells its debts gets a cash advance on its debts thus reducing the time for waiting cash collections from its debtors,

b. Time-value of money is taken into consideration. While the company could have waited longer to collects its money, with debt factoring, the funds are collected immediately.

c. The company will be relieved of cash flow constraints.

d. There is cost reduction in terms of credit administration. Few staff need to be involved in credit recording and so there are less staff costs. Most of the credit administration work will be done by the factoring company.

e. There is a greater possibility of having no bad debts as are debts are sold. The only cost is commission fee paid to the factoring company.

13.8   Other methods of debt collection

Apart from debt factoring, another method of collecting debts is to use the debt collection agents. Debt Collection agents is a common method whereby a third party organization agrees to collect debts on your behalf on commission basis. The difference between debt factoring and agents is that the debt collectors do not pay you any cash advance but they employ different strategies to collect money from your debtors,and at the end you have to pay them the commission . The commission is based on a percentage of the amount collected . However, sometimes the use of debt collecting agents is not a most preferable method because they are considered not to be friendly with customers, they may use harsh methods that can harass your customers. The use of debt collection agents might erode the relationship with your customers and can force them to terminate their business relationship .

13.9   Conclusion

Survival of companies in business depends so much on the abiliy to manage debtors. If debtors are not managed, company might experience problems in its cash flow and if the problem continues it migh lead to insorvency. This chapter has higlighted the importance of good credit policy as one way of ensuring that debts are managed properly to avoid the problems assocaited with non-correction of funds from debtors. It has discussed the advtanges, disadvtanges of credit policy and the variables of the good credit policy. Furthermore, he chapter highilights on the startegies which management can use to improve debt collection

Practice Questions

Question 1

Discuss the factors that you will consider when formulating your company credit policy?

Question 2

The development of a credit policy in a business organization is a crucial element for effective management of working capital. In view of your company/institution, evaluate the relevance and applicability of credit policy and prepare your company credit policy.

Question 3

(a) Timothy Ltd is a manufacturing company based in Tanzania which manufactures a range of products from raw materials. These are stored in wherever space is available in the factory and operatives help themselves to what they require. S et out the undesirable consequences which you would expect to occur in this policy

(b) What would you expect to be the elements of an efficient credit control policy? Indicate the likely consequences of a policy which is too tight and of a policy with is too loose.

Question 4

In this modern globalized world, we should have uniform credit policies. Do you agree? Why or why not?

CHAPTER 14

STOCK MANAGEMENT

14.1   Introduction

Stock Management in itself is a discipline which needs to be explored in- depth. However, for the purpose of helping non-financial managers, it is not my intention to create confusion with theories related to stock management but rather hope to give basic knowledge that is useful in day to day management functions. With the presence of stock management experts in organizations, managers with an understanding of the following issues that I will discuss they can perform much better than having no knowledge at all.

Stock management addresses one component of a company's current assets which appear on a balance sheet. Stocks are a critical component of company assets and mismanagement of stocks can cause many problems to a company. There are costs which a company will incur if stocks are not managed well so it is important for managers to give weight to stock management and to provide support to employees whose expertise is this.

14.2   Stock management problems in organizations

There are number of stock management problems which Chief Excutive Managers should be aware of them in order for them o design specific strategies to address them. The folowing are the common problems in stock management:

a. **Corruption** through collusion with suppliers, inflated prices, etc. Also, compromising on quality and the existance of ghost suppliers
b. **Pilferage** of stock through loss or theft.
c. **Overstocking** items that are not needed at the time and just tie up capital without benefit.
d. **Under-stocking** because of a lack of available stocks, lack of capital or ignorance of market fluctuations.
e. **Lack of Skills to manage and control stocks** resulting from inadequate and untrained staff who cannot effective manage the organization's stock
f. **Lack of stock management systems** or systems of poor stock recording especially when using manual systems.
g. **Keeping obsolete stock.**
h. **Dead Stock** resulting from holding on to items that don't move or move slowly.
i. **Stock deterioration**
j. **Procurement of expired stock**
k. **Delays in procurement** due to bureaucracy
l. **Lack of effective procurement policies**
m. **Ignoring procurement policies** (where procurement policies exist)
n. **Holding stock for speculation** reasons
o. **Buying or holding on to outdated technology**
p. **Inadequate storage space**
q. **Lack of skilled manpower**
r. **Inadequate machinery** for managing stock
s. **Lack of knowledge** of enforcement laws
t. **Disorganized procurement planning**
u. **Poor tenders advertisement**
v. **Non-compliance with contract** awards, procedures, and criteria
w. **Weak administrative review and complaints processes**

14.3   Effective stock management at the company level

The above listed problems are common in most private African businesses as well as in the public sector but when addressed, companies will have much more effective stock management-- a critical factor in financial success. The recommendations below are not all-inclusive but are suggestions which may help address stock problems:

a.   Improve stock control
b.   Apply stock control models
c.   Use a computerized inventory system
d.   Train staff in effective stock management
e.   Improve staff morale to avoid theft and corruption
f.   Create and utilize a clear stock management policy
g.   Establish proper warehouses

14.4   Requirements for successful stock management

As already mentioned, stock is a critical component of current assets of any company and so managers need to recognize the importance of quality stock management. Poor stock management can lead to financial disaster. Effective stock management requires the manager to:

- *Manage the costs related to stock procurement and handling.* Costs of procuring and handling stock should be kept at a minimum.
- *Ensure that there are no stock shortages.* Stock shortages often lead to other financial problems and may affect the production process in case of manufaturing companies
- *Ensure that there is no excess stock* which tie up company funds and lead to low cash problems.

It is therefore important to note that failures in stock management can result in many negative consequences for your company. Let us review some consequences resulting from too much or too little stock.

Consequences of maintaining too much stock

There are consequences of mantaining too much stocks to organizations. A number of those consequences are mentioned below:

- ➢ Excess capital is tied up unproductively in stock
- ➢ Funds may be wasted on extra storage
- ➢ Increased Insurance costs for the stock
- ➢ Stock my deteriorate or lose value when kept in storage long term
- ➢ Changes in demand or technology may result in stock wastage

Consequences of maintaining too little stock

Mantaining too little stock have also some consequences which inlude the following :

- ➢ Production may be interrupted due to stock shortage
- ➢ Frequenting ordering may be necessary and may incur additional costs
- ➢ Bulk buying discounts are missed

14.5   Management of stock costs

The manager concerned should ensure that stock costs are kept at a minimum. If stock costs are not managed, there are consequences such as those mentioned above. There are three types of costs which we need to understand in order to know how to manage them. These costs can have greater negative impact on the organization if they are overlooked.

1. Holding Costs or Carrying Costs- These are costs incurred by the company after procuring these stocks such as warehousing costs and insurance costs. The more you procure goods you are likely to incur these type of costs.
2. Procuring costs or Ordering Costs- These are costs of procuring the goods such as the clerical costs incurred

3.   Stock –out Costs- When a company goes out of stock and it needs to keep its production capacity or maintain the supply to the customer it will have to incur extra costs to buy the requiredstock. Going out of stock might lead to the loss of customers as they will have to seek another supplier.

Managing the above costs requires us to understand how to use stock models to estimate the optimal order amount for each stocked item, to make decisions on whether to agree to a bulk order discount, to decide what optimum re-order level is for each stocked item and to determine how frequently orders should placed through determining the best stock turnover rate.

Economic Order Quantity (EOQ) model

One of the models we can use to minimize stock costs is a deterministic model called Economic Order Quantity (EOQ Model). This model is deemed deterministic because the parameters used are known with certainty and can be easily predicted. The EOQ promotes ordering quantities which minimize total ordering and holding costs. To calculate the EOQ, the following assumptions should be considered:

a.   There are known, constant stock holding costs;
b.   There are known, constant ordering costs;
c.   The rates of demand are known;
d.   Price per unit is constant;
e.   Whole batches are delivered at once;
f.   No stock outs are allowed.

The following formula is used to determine the Economic Order Quantity:

$$EOQ = \frac{\sqrt{2CD}}{\sqrt{C_c}}$$

Where
C = Ordering cost per order
D = Annual demand
Cc = Carrying costs or holding costs per unit

Example

ABC Ltd uses 500,000 rolls of toilet paper per annum which are $10 each to purchase. The ordering and handling costs are $1.5 per order and carrying costs are 15% per annum.

(a) Calculate the E.O.Q.
(b) How many orders should be ordered per annum?
(c) Calculate the annual ordering costs
(d) Calculate the Annual Holding Costs
(e) Calculate the Total costs

Solution

(a) Given:
Annual Demand (D) = 500,000 toilet papers
Carrying Costs (Cc) = 15% of $ 10
Ordering Costs per Unit = $ 1.5

$$EOQ = \sqrt{\frac{2CD}{Cc}}$$

$$= \sqrt{\frac{2 \times 1.5 \times 500,000}{0.15 \times 1}}$$

$$= \sqrt{\frac{1500,000}{0.15}}$$

$$= 3,162 \text{ Rolls of toilet paper}$$

(b) Numbers of orders needed per year

$$= \frac{\text{Annual Demand}}{\text{EOQ}}$$

$$= \frac{500,000}{3162}$$

$$= 158 \text{ Orders needed}$$

(c) Ordering Costs

Ordering Costs = Number of Orders x Ordering Costs per order

$$= 158 \times 1.5$$
$$= \$ 237$$

(d) Holding Costs

Since we do not hold the stock permanently in our stores, we need to find the average needed stock to hold in storage and multiply by the holding cost per unit to determine the total annual holding costs

$$\text{Holding Costs} = \text{EOQ}/2 \times 0.15$$
$$= 3162/2 \times 0.15$$
$$= \$ 237.15$$

(e) Total stock costs

Purchasing Costs + Ordering Costs + Holding Costs
500,000(10) + 237 + 237 = \$ 5,000,474

14.6 Public procurement issues and ethics

Ensuring stock procurement is for success in managing the current assets of the organization and is an important role for managers. As a matter of advice, managers should ensure that their staff are aware of and adhere to the proper ethical standards. They should never use their title for personal gain and should seek to uphold the organization's standing in all purchasing policies by maintaining the highest standards of integrity in all business relationships both inside and outside company. Managers should also foster professional competence by complying with the letter and spirit of the law, of professional guidance, and of contractual obligations and should reject any business practices which might reasonably be deemed improper. Managers should work to optimize the use of resources they are responsible for to the greatest benefit of the company.

In dealing with customers, all deals should be handled professionally and ethically. Managers should generally avoid overly-friendly approaches which suppliers may misinterpret and try to exploit in the future. Managers should also avoid conflict of interest situations in which future decision-making could be compromised. There are other areas of consideration especially when the manager has direct influence over procurement functions and some are outlined below.

> **Supplier's gifts:** It is not ethical for civil servants or managers in their official capacity to accept any gift or consideration as an inducement or reward for doing or refraining from doing anything; or showing favor or disfavor to any supplier.
> **Hospitality from suppliers:** Managers can accept modest hospitality from suppliers such as diaries, calendars, and modest lunches. However, these should be infrequent and should never be allowed to reach a position where your impartiality may be influenced or be perceived to be influenced.
> **Collusions with suppliers:** Occasionally managers collude with suppliers to steal company resources which is, obviously, not ethical and is corrupt.

14.7   Professionalism in dealing with suppliers

Managers are not always the only people dealing with suppliers so they must also monitor interactions between their employees and suppliers. The following are some of the professional ways which should be encouraged in dealings with suppliers:

- Honesty
- Fairness
- Impartiality
- No discrimination based on race, sex, religion or other factors
- Suppliers should not be misled in supplying your company
- The legitimate interests of both the supplier and company should be recognized throughout the negotiation and administration of contracts
- Casual enquiries from purchasers to suppliers for prices should be avoided and all requests should be based on a serious intention to purchase

14.8   Need for inventory management policies

Major companies operating with large stock and large amounts of money need to have a sound and clear inventory management policy. The main objectives of inventory management could include the following:

a.   To ensure compliance with generally-accepted accounting principles through a uniform policy regarding capitalization and valuation of stock,

b.   To establish procedures for the management and control of stock,

c.   To establish procedures as related to procurement, receipts, issuing and recording of company stock,

d.   To establish proper guidelines on disposal of company assets.

14.9   Scope of the Inventory Policy

The scope of the policy will depend on the size of the organization, types of inventory it handles, as well as the environment and number of staff responsible for inventory management. However, the following issues should be addressed by any stock management policy:

- Types of company stocks should be clearly stated
- Which documents will be used for recording, receipts, and other stages of the management process
- Clearly established rules for authorization, approval for procurement and disposal of inventory
- Designation of a clear custodian of inventory
- Procedures for lost or stolen property
- Disposal Procedures
- What Valuations method will be used to value stock at the end of the year

The above mentioned issues are should guide companies but managers may need to consider other aspects as well.

14.10   Conclusion

Stock management is a cruacial aspect which management should take it seriously otherwise the organization incur extra costs and hence reduce profitability. To manage stocks efficiently it requires a grasp of knowledge that can help in the management process. This topic has tried to underscore the important aspects of stock management by explaining what really entails effective stock management and the problems related to stock management. The chapter has discussed how to deal with stock supliers to ensure adequate supply and availability of stock and has also explained different types of stock costs, the need for stock management policy and the scope management the policy.

Practice Questions

Question 1

Discuss the major stock related problems in your company and possible reasons for these problems. What recommendations could you make to alleviate the problems?

Question 2

What are potential consequences of having a stock management policy in your company?

Question 3

Discuss how the introduction of computer hardware and software can help improve stock management in a modern business.

Question 4

The assumptions in the EOQ cannot be applicable in a hyper-inflation economy where prices are not constant. Do you agree? Why or why not?

Question 5

How can managers increase ethical behavior in stock procurement functions at the company level?

CHAPTER 15

MANAGEMENT OF THE FINANCIAL ACCOUNTING AND FINANCIAL REPORTING FUNCTION

15.1 Introduction

The accounting function is one of the most critical functions of any organization as it deals with the handling and tracking of financial resources. Management should understand that mishandling the accounting function could result in serious financial resource losses which could jeorpadize the operations of the organization. It is the responsibility of management to ensure that there is a skilled accounting department that can be appropriately responsible for recording all business transactions undertaken by the organization compiling these transactions into clear reports. Financial statements are important to help management in decision-making so their accuracy is paramount.

15.2 The Role of management in enhancing the accounting and reporting function

Management can do several things to enhance the accounting and financial reporting for their organizations. The following are the key roles which management can play in order to ensure that the accounting and reporting aspects of their of organizational transactions is carried out correctly:

1. **Recruitment:** Management has the sole responsibility of recruiting appropriate staff for accounting and financial functions. Recruitment need to be done skillfully and the vetting of senior staff such as finance managers and accountants should not be ignored. Proper qualifications such as diplomas in accounting and higher qualifications such as CPA certificates are importnat when recruiting accountants and finance managers. Membership of staff in accounting professional bodies should be a must for Chief Accountants and Finance Managers.

2. **Staffing**: Management should ensure that the department responsible for accounting functions is properly staffed. Understaffing can lead to delayed reporting and erraneous errors because staff are overwhelmed.

3. **Proper segregation of accounting functions:** Management should ensure that there is proper segregation of accounting functions to avoid the overriding of internal controls put in place, minimize errors and the occurrence of fraud.

4. **Capacity Building and Training:** The accounting profession is a dynamic profession which requires accountants to be updated with changes that are taking place. New international reporting standards are being established from time to time. Management should support accountants by sending them to training in order for them to keep up in a the global arena.

5. **Support**: Management should provide support to accounting personnel in order to help them fulfill their responsibilities. Support include technical and administation support too otherwise staff might not fulfill their responsibilities effectively. Management should facilitate the computerization of the accounting systems as the use of manual accounting system is no longer relevant in modern business organizations.

6. **Motivation**: Personnel dealing with accounting functions need to be motivated in order for them to fulfill their work effeciently. The motivation has to be based on more than than financial benefits.

Staff should be encouraged to gain additional certifications and should be recognized for professional accomplishments in public setting.

7. **Proper renumeration:** In order to establish a stong accounting department, management has to ensure that accountants are renumerated in line with their qualifications. This will help maintain consistency of staff.

15.3   Need for a computerized accounting system to enhance the accounting function

In modern business organizations, the accounting functions are facilitated by having in place a proper computerized accounting systems to avoid the use of manual systems which is prone for much errors and time consuming to process the accounting information. Management should consider a number of factors when making a decision to procure or change accounting software.

Delone (1988) explains that before deciding about computerizing, the company should have a solid and effective accounting system in place. Computerizing a weak system will not suddenly improve it. There are correct and incorrect reasons to computerize accounting systems.

Some poor reasons to computerize accounting systems are:

(a) All companies have computerized their systems except us!
(b) The accountants are not doing well. We should computerize everything!
(c) We have enough money to buy the computer and software!
(d) We have received donated computers and so we should computerize!

Good reasons for computerizing the accounting systems should be based on a clear cost-benefit analysis. If the benefits of computerization are high, then companies should be willing to invest more in the process. Even when the benefits are expected to be greater than the costs of the software, there are still issues to consider before buying in:

1. **Scalability:** The ability of the package to meet future financial accounting needs as the company grows. Buying a package that will only address the company's present accounting needs will cost more for the company in the future when accounting needs will have increased. For example, a company may purchase a program which can only accommodate nine-digit revenues but as the company grows, if they pass that threshold, the software becomes useless. Although it may be more expensive, companies should buy their accounting software with a visualization of the business in 3-5 years' time in mind. Software that is easily upgraded are also highly recommended as upgrades will cause minimal disruption and costs to the business in the future.

2. **Support from Software Suppliers:** It is advisable to procure software from local vendors who are licensed by the suppliers of accounting packages so that technical support as needed. Licensed vendors normally provide support in terms of training staff how to use the package and solving technical problems which might arise when using the package.

3. **Ease of use:** The accounting package sought by the organization should be easy to use. It is important that a demo package is tried and tested before buying the package. Companies should also consider if the package can interact/integrate with other software that you are using.

4. **Software features needed by the organization:** Most accounting software packages come with several features. Some accounting packages include modules for inventory, foreign exchange, consolidations and others. Remember to buy a package that has what you need now and in the foreseeable future but don't invest money in large packages full of unneeded features. The number of users allowed and types of reports that can be produced are very important considerations when buying new software.

5. **Accountant Interface:** Since the responsibility of handling the company accounts belongs to the company itself, it is important that accountants are involved in the process from beginning to end. The accountant is an important person in helping to supply

answers as to what type of package is needed. Such questions could be: what types of reports do we need?

Whatsoftware are the accountants used to working with and what do they prefer? Can the package generate the required reports without additional work?

6. **Availability of qualified staff:** One major consideration before purchasing software is whether the organization has staff capable of utilizing the package. There may be a need to employ qualified staff or train up current staff. Another option could be to use part-time staff to use the software. The disadvantage of this is that part-time staff may not stay at the organization long-term and then accounts can get backlogged while looking for a new trained or trainable staff person.

15.4   Conclusion

Accounting is the foundation of having proper financial statements that are useful for various financial decisions that Chief Executives have to make. The accounting function involves the recording of all business transactions. A proper accounting system which is supported with appropriate number of staff with the skills and knowledge to support proper financial reporting. This topic explains what role management should playing enhancing the accounting and reporting function and why is important to set-up a computerized accounting system in order to enhance the accounting function. The chapter provides advice about what factors management should consider when deciding to computerize the accounting systems or changing the existing computerized system.

Practice Questions

Question 1

What factors should management consider when computerizing the accounting function?

Question 2

What role should management to ensure that a company has an effective financial accounting and reporting function?

Question 3

Discuss the consequences of poor financial accounting and reporting function to the organization.

CHAPTER 16

UNDERSTANDING FINANCIAL STATEMENTS

16.1 Introduction

Financial statements are derived from the financial accounting discipline. This is the end result of the accounting process. When the accounting system is working properly and all accounting principles discussed in the previous chapter have been applied, the financial statements are will provide relevant and reliable information to various users thus helping them to make sound economic decisions.

Financial statements include the statement of financial position (balance sheet), comprehensive statement of income, and the statement of cash flow. The preparation of financial statements need to be backed by accounting policies and company directors' report before they are distributed to the users. It is also mandatory that financial statements must be audited before the distribution and therefore the auditor's report becomes a part of financial statements. Auditing, in this case, is important to give an opinion on whether the financial statements are prepared in accordance to accounting standards and whether they give a true and fair view of the organization's financial affairs. We will discuss the individual components of financial statements in the next sections of this chapter.

It very important for managers to ensure that the financial accounting system of their organization is strong because this is where all sources of information for preparation of the financial statements originate. In the case of a weak accounting system, the financial statements prepared by this system will be questionable. Strengthening might require proper recruitment of staff, training, good remuneration packages and the use of modern information technology such as computers and good accounting software.

16.2   Regulatory Framework for Preparation of Financial Statements

The preparation of financial statements is guided by International Financial Reporting Standards (IFRS) which are issued by the International Accounting Standard Board (IASB). The application of the standards is now a global issue because of the need for harmonization of accounting practice. Prior to harmonization of financial reporting standards, each country accounting board issued its own guidelines and standards on how financial statements were to be prepared. In African countries there is still a major problem as very few companies have incorporated IFRS in preparation of their financial statements. A number of projects and studies have been carried out by national accounting bodies with support from the World Bank to ensure that companies and government agencies adapt their financial statement requirements to fall in line with international financial reporting standards.

There are financial reporting standards for different business operations and managers should understand that standards might not be static in the long-term because changes in the global economy can occur at any time. The major question here is to understand why the harmonization of accounting standards has taken place. A few reasons mentioned below have led to the creation of harmonized accounting standards:

a.   Drive towards globalization
b.   The need to harmonize training of accounting professionals
c.   An increase in international business worldwide

16.3 Users of Financial Statements

Financial statements prepared in accordance to international accounting standards and principles are very useful to different kinds of users. Statements can be used to derive relevant information for specific needs and so it is very important for accountants to prepare the statements with consideration of their needs. The following are the main users of financial statements and their specific needs in financial statements:

The Government and its agencies

The government needs companies' financial statements for the purpose of determining the profit of companies which is subject to payment of taxation. It is through the financial statements that companies' profits or losses can be ascertained and, from there, taxation can be charged by the government. When the government is funder for the organization, the government will be interested in the allocation of resources and the organization or business' activities. Governments, through the use of financial statements, can easily regulate business and organization activities.

Lenders

Most lenders of funds will be check financial statements to see if prospective borrowers will be able to pay back borrowed money with interest. Through the financial statements, they will be able to determine the cash flow and liquidity ratios as well as the times earned interest rate. This information will help them decide whether to give loans or not based on predictions about borrowers' ability to payback.

Shareholders

Shareholders will utilize financial statements to determine the return of their risk capital invested in the business. They will also want to see how much return is made by the company and what will be returned to them through dividends.

The Employees

In many profit-making business organizations and non-profit organizations, financial statements are restricted to specific people in the organization. They are treated as highly-confidential and so sharing them with all employees might not be practical. However, employees should have access to financial statements so that they understand the stability and profitability of their employers so as to assess the entity's ability to pay salaries and retirement benefits. If financial statements are shared with employees, managers should provide some explanation so that misunderstandings do not occur.

Suppliers and other Trade creditors

Suppliers of goods on credit will view financial statements to see if the company will be able to pay off any debts in the future. Suppliers and other trade creditors may also be refused access to financial statements because of confidentiality rules. In some countries, only certain companies in specific industries are required to publish their financial statements for public viewing. Other businesses do not publish their financial statements and so suppliers and other trade creditors may not have access to all financial statements they desire.

Customers

Customers may be interested in information about the continuance of an entity, especially when they have long –term involvement with, or are dependent on. The publication of accounts in newspapers by banks operating in most African countries now, is a new paradigm that protects customers against loss of money in banks. It can be argued that this protection clause will protect only the elite group which understand the role of financial statements while others continue banking with poor performing banks because of ignorance. African governments should invest time in educating citizens on the role of financial statements.

Investors

Investors are providers of risk capital. Prospective investors are concerned with the return provided by their investments. They need information from financial statements to help them make decisions about whether they should buy, hold or sell their shares. Under normal circumstances prospective investors' should be able read and interpret financial statements so that they make sound financial decisions.

16.4   The purpose of Financial Statements

There are three major purposes as to why we need to prepare financial statements and each of these purposes is clearly explained through components of the financial statements. The main purposes are: determining the financial position of the organization, determining the profitability performance of the organization, and determining the changes in cash flow.

16.5   Determining the financial position of an organization

The financial position of an organization is represented by its assets as well as its equity and liabilities. These three major items are represented in the common accounting equation. The accounting equation is stated as follows:

$$ASSETS = EQUITY + LIABILITIES$$

Left hand side of the equation

The left hand side of the accounting equation represents the assets of the business owner.

Assets

These represent where funds are invested. It is also good at this stage to mention that the assets which the business owner puts his money into can be grouped into different categories

1. **Fixed Assets– Non-current assets**

   These are assets whose life time is more than one year. They are considered more durable and of higher value. Another characteristic of fixed assets is that they are not easily convertible to cash and they involve large amounts of money. Examples of fixed assets include land and buildings, machinery, motor vehicles, computers, aircrafts, ships and equipment.

2. **Current Assets**

   These are the assets whose life time is less than two years. It can also include assets which can quickly and easily being converted into cash. Examples of current assets are cash, trade debtors (accounts receivables), stock (inventory) and pre-payments.

3. **Investments**

   The grouping of assets into two major groups is not conclusive as recently a new group of assets has been introduced. These are investments which used to be grouped as either fixed or current assets depending on the duration of the investment. The international accounting standards now require investments to be grouped separately as, 'investments'. Examples of investments include various fixed deposits accounts, investments in subsidiaries, commercial papers and other financial instruments.

4. **Intangible Assets**

   These are assets which cannot be physically seen but exist as they have underlying value such as the copyrights and trade patents

Right hand side of the accounting equation

The right hand side of the accounting equation is represented by owners' equity plus retained earnings and liabilities. Owner's equity plus liabilities shows where the funding for assets came from.

Owner's equity

Owner's equity or capital is the money from the owner himself/herself. In order to start a business, the owner chooses to invest his own saved money as business capital.

Retained Earnings

As businesses grow, they begin making profit. The owner might then decide, instead of taking the profit for personal use, to re-invest that money into the business. The portion of profits retained in the business through this manner are called retained earnings, which become part of capital.

Liabilities

Liabilities represent what is owed by the business owner/organization to others. These people or companies whom the owner owes expect that their money will be returned at some future date. In case their money is not returned according to the agreement, they have a right to take legal actions. In other words, these people provide additional funds which to finance the purchases of assets which the owner is unable to fund from his/her own sources.

Liabilities can also be grouped as short-term or long-term liabilities depending on the time required for paying back the liability. Short-term liabilities must be paid back in on year or less. Examples of these are the trade creditors (accounts payables), bank overdrafts and accrual charges.

Long-term liability payoffs require more than one year and include debentures and mortgages. Long-term liabilities have fixed charges that are attached with interest repayment, which must be paid annually or semi-annually.

Understanding the statement of financial position (Balance Sheet)

The accounting equation discussed above reflects the financial position of a business organization. However, this equation can be explained by the use of the balance sheet in a very clear manner to include details of assets, liabilities and owner's equity.

The balance sheet, in a practical sense, is just a statement showing the accounting equation but for learning purposes, we can draw a balance sheet in a T- format where there are two sides. One of the sides should represent the assets (let's say the left hand side) and the other side (let's say the right hand side) will represent the owner's equity and liabilities. Readers should not be confused when reading an American book or British book in regards to the right presentation of the balance sheet. Americans will show assets on the left side of the balance sheet while owner's equity and liabilities on the right hand side while the Britons will do the opposite. Which side represents what has no effect on the equation. For purpose of learning, the T- format may be relevant but in real business practices, financial statements including the balance sheet should be presented in statement format.

In practice the preparation of a balance sheet depends accurate recording of transactions as recorded and calculated by accounting staff which results in the creation of a trial balance. The trial balance will show the end balance of each category of accounts including assets, equity and liabilities. Once these balances are available, accountants can prepare financial statements. It is, therefore, important for managers to ensure that the accounting function is highly supported so that all business transactions are properly recorded and high quality financial statements can be created. If the accounting function is delayed, inaccurate or inefficient, financial statements including the balance sheet are likely to contain errors. In preparing the balance sheet, the balancing of the accounting equation should be a guiding principle.

We have to, then, understand that when the balance sheet is in balance, it doesn't actually mean that everything is correct. There are times that a balance is found with mistakes embedded in the equation. If principles of accounting discussed in the previous chapter, for example, are not incorporated, the balance sheet can still balance but with errors.

Example

The following lists of balances were extracted from the books of Faith Ltd, a company specializing in art promotion, as of 30th Sept 2019. Capital $200, 000, Trade debtors $20,000, Cash $134,000, Stock $25,000, Investment $100,000, 8% Debenture $100,000, Bank Overdraft $85,000, Net Profit $10,000, Short-term loan $164,000, Building $200,000, Motor Vehicle $150,000 and Accrued Charges $70,000.

Use these balances to prepare a balance sheet for 30th Sept 2019

Solution

GWANA WANE LTD BALANCE SHEET AS AT 30TH SEPT 2019

Owners Equity + Liabilities	USD	Fixed Assets	USD
Capital	200,000	Building	200,000
Net Profit	10,000	Motor Vehicle	150,000
	210,000		
Liabilities		Investments	100,000
8% Debenture	100,000	**Current Assets**	
Bank Overdraft	85,000	Cash	134,000
Short Term Loan	164,000	Stock	25,000
Accrued Charges	70,000	Debtors	20,000
	629,000		**629,000**

The above T-format balance sheet is common in classroom setup when individuals are learning financial statements for the first time. In parctice, using a balance sheet in T-format is not prefera ble. As per international accounting standards, the balance sheet is translated to a Statement of Financial Position. This statement will show the assets of the orerganization and how these assets are represented by owner's equity and liabilities. For example, the above balance sheet will look as a follows:

GWANA WANE LTD STATEMENT OF FINANCIAL POSITION AS AT 30ᵀᴴ SEPT 2019

Fixed Assets	USD	
Building		200,000
Motor Vehicle		150,000
Investments		100,000
Current Assets		
Cash		134,000
Stock		25,000
Debtors		20,000
		629,000

Represented by :

Owners Equity + Liabilities	USD	
Capital		200,000
Net Profit		10,000
		210,000
Liabilities		
8% Debenture		100,000
Bank Overdraft		85,000
Short Term Loan		164,000
Accrued Charges		70,000
		629,000

16.6 Determining the profitability performance of an organization

Another purpose of preparing financial statement is to determine the performance of the organization in terms of profitability during the trading period. Normally profitability is measured by determining the net profit and net loss of the organization during a specified period. Profitability is easily reflected in the comprehensive income statement which is part of the financial statement. Another name for the comprehensive income statement is profit and loss account.

Understanding the comprehensive Income Statement

The income statement will show all income and expenditures during the trading period and the difference between the two is either net profit or net loss. The net profit or loss is a book figure arrived by taking net income and deducting all operating expenditures of the business during the reporting period. However, for clear understanding on determining the net income/profit, the following is the proper format of presenting the income statement:

AX Ltd

Comprehensive Income Statement for the Period Ending 30th Sept 2019

Sales	xxxx
Less : Cost of Goods Sold	(xxxx)
Gross Profit	xxxx
Less: Operating Expenses/Adm Costs	(xxxx)
Net Profit before interest and Taxes	xxxxx
Less : Interest Expenses	(xxxx)
Net Profit after taxes	**xxxx**

Note:

The net profit after tax is the amount available for distribution to shareholders in form of dividends. The decision to distribute dividends depends on the dividend policy of the company. The option can be either to distribute part of profits or to have nil distribution in that year when the company has made profits or not due to various factors including the problem of cash flow or the need to re-invest back the money into business.

Determination of Cost of Sales

Cost of sales is determined by taking the opening stock (at cost) at the beginning of trading period, adding to it the net purchases costs and, thereafter, deducting the closing stock (at cost) at the end of the trading period. The term 'net purchases' needs special attention-- there are times when you buy goods from suppliers some goods might be damaged or not to the quality standard you require and you may then return them to the supplier. In order to arrive at the correct figure of net purchase,s the value of goods returned to supplier will need to be deducted from the purchases figure.

The following format will guide you on how to determine the cost of goods sold:

Cost of Goods sold computation

Opening Stock		xxxxx
Add: Purchases	xxxx	
Returns Outward	(xxx)	
Net Purchases		xxxxx
Goods available for Sale		xxxxxx
Less: Closing Stock		(xxxx)
Cost of goods sold		**xxxxxx**

Gross Profit

This is the profit arising from the typical trading of the goods. It is found by comparing the net sales and the cost of goods sold. The gross profit is created from buying the goods and selling the goods before deducting other operating expenses. Only expenses that are related directly to buying the goods can be included in the calculations of gross profit. Where goods sold to customers are returned due to various factors, they need not be included in the sales figure as they will tarnish the sales figure. Therefore, to calculate net sales you must deduct the value of goods returned by customers from total sales.

Net Profit

This is a profit remaining with the organization after operating expenses are deducted from the gross profit figure. All operating expenditures during the trading period need be matched with the total revenue arising from sales and other miscellaneous revenues so as to arrive at the net profit figure. It is important to note that the principle of matching is applied in order to arrive at the correct net profit figure. The net profit figure is an indicator of profitability performance of the organization.

Illustration 1

The following balances are extracted from the books of ABC Ltd as on 31st Dec 2010. All figures are in US dollars.

From these balances, prepare the comprehensive income Statement.

Sales	20,000,000
Purchases	10,000,000
Returns Inward	4,000,000
Returns Outward	2,000,000
Sales and Wages	1,000,000
Opening Stock	2,500,000
Closing Stock	4,600,000
Admininstrative Expenses	2,000,000
Auditing Fees	1,000,000
Bad Debts	500,000
Bank Charges	600,000
Loan interest Expenses	100,000
Debtors	400,000
Share Capital	600,000

The country corporation tax rate is 30%.

Solution

ABC LTD
INCOME AND EXPENDITURE STATEMENT
FOR THE YEAR ENDED 31st DEC 2007

Sales	20,000,000	
Less: Returns inward	4,000,000	16,000,000
Cost of Goods Sold		
Opening Stock	2,500,000	
Add: Purchases	10,000,000	
	12,500,000	
Less : Returns Outwartd	2,000,000	
Goods available for sale	10,500,000	
Less: Closing Stock	4,600,000	
Cost of Goods sold		5,100,000
GrossProfits		**10,100,000**
Less: Adm and Overhead costs		
Salaries and Wages	1,000,000	
Administrative Expenses	2,000,000	
Auditing Fees	1,000,000	
Bad debts	500,000	
Bank Charges	600,000	
		5,100,000
Net profit before Taxes and Interest		**5,000,000**
Expenses		100,000
Less: Interest Expenses		
Net profit before taxes		4,900,000
Less : Taxation (30%)		1,470,000
Net profit after taxes		**3,430,000**

Determining changes in cash flow

Another purpose for the preparation of financial statement is to explain changes that have taken place with cash flow during a reporting period.

This can only be achieved by preparing a, 'Cash flow Statement". A cash flow statement shows where an institution's cash is coming from and how it is being used over a period of time.

A cash flow statement classifies the cash flow originating from operating, investing and financing activities.

- *Operating activities:* services provided (income-earning activities).
- *Investing activities:* expenditures that have been made for resources intended to generate future income and cash flow.
- *Financing activities:* resources obtained from and resources returned to the owners, resources obtained through borrowings (short-term or long-term) as well as donor funds.

Notes to the Accounts

The notes to the accounts are part and parcel of financial statements. Through the notes, company policies impacting the preparation of the statements are clearly explained. Issues such as the depreciation policy and the accounting policy as well as details of schedules of computations are provided. Details of major balances in the financial statements are also given.

16.7   Responsibility for preparation of financial statements

The responsibility for preparing financial statements for the organization rests with the management and not with external auditors. The management has the sole responsibility of ensuring that all books of accounts are kept in order and that all business transactions are properly recorded. The final accounts must be prepared in accordance to accepted international accounting standards before they are submitted for auditing by the external auditors. However, in some cases, small company's accounts may be prepared by the same professionals who do the auditing. This scenario is not recommended because it removes the auditor's independence.

16.8   Qualitative factors of financial statements

The best financial statement presentations consider both quantitative and qualitative factors. The qualitative factors are the attributes that make the information provided in the financial statements useful to different users. The following are attributes which should be considered by companies preparing financial statements:

Clarity

Financial statements must be prepared in such a way that they can be understood by the users. If users cannot understand the content and logic of these statements then they are of no use to them.

Relevance

Information provided by the financial statement must be relevant so as to prevent misleading decisions.

Reliability

Financial statements' information must be reliable to users. The reliability depends on the evidence used to prepare the financial statements.

Comparability

The financial statements of an organization must be capable of being compared with financial statements of other companies operating in the same business or industry over a period of time. Comparisons also can be made within the same organization but over a period of time. This is only possible if principles of accounts are observed during the preparation of the statements (such as the use of the consistency principle).

Comprehensive Question

The following list of balances were extracted from the books of Ngo'nga Limited on 28th February 2019

LIST OF BALANCES AS AT 28TH FEB 2019

Particulars	Dr	Cr
Purchases	11,280	
Sales		19,740
Cash at Bank	1,140	
Cash in Hand	210	
Capital		9,900
Drawings	2,850	
Office Furniture	1,440	
Rent	1,020	
Wages and Salaries	2,580	
Discount Allowed	690	
Discount Received		360
Stock (1st Feb 2018)	2,970	
Debtors	4,920	
Creditors		2,490
Provision for Bad Debts		270
Delivery Van	2,400	
Van Running Costs	450	
Bad Debts wriiten Off	810	
	32760	**32760**

Notes

1. Stock on 28th Feb 2019 $ 3,510
2. Wages and Salaries accrued $ 90
3. Rent Prepaid $140
4. Van Running Costs Owing at 28th Feb 2019. $ 60
5. Increase Provision for Bad debts by $ 60
6. Provide for depreciation as follows :
    Office Furniture $ 180
    Delivery Van $ 480.

Required

a. Prepare the Comprehensive income sttaement of Ngonga for the period ended 28th Feb 2019
b. Prepare the statement of financial position as at 28th Feb 2019

Solution

NGONGA'S

COMPREHENSIVE INCOME STATEMENT FOR THE YEAR ENDED 28TH FEB 2019

Sales		19,740
Less: Cost of Sales		
Opening stock	2,970	
Add: Purchases	11,280	
	14,250	
Less: Closing Stock	(3,510)	10,740
GROSS PROFIT		**9,000**
Other Incomes		
Discount Received		360
		9,360
Less: Operating Costs		
Wages and Salaries (2580+90)	2,670	
Rent (1020-140)	880	
Discounts Allowed	690	
Van Running Costs (450+60)	510	
Bad Debts (810+60)	870	
Depreciation		
Office Furniture	180	
Delivery Van	480	6,280
NET PROFIT		**3,080**

NGONGA'S
STATEMENT OF FINANCIAL POSITION
AS AT 28ᵀᴴ FEBRUARY 2019

Fixed Assets

Office Furniture	1,440	
Less: Depreciation	180	1,260
Delivery Van	2,400	
Less: Depreciation	480	1,920
Current Assets		
Cash at BANK	1,140	
Cash in Hand	210	
Debtors	4,920	
Less: Provision for Bad Debts	330	4,590
Stock		3,510
Prepaid Expenses		140	9,590
		12,770

Represented by
Equity + Liabilities

Capital	9,900	
Add: Net Profit	3,080	
	12,980	
Less: Drawings	2,850	10,130
Current Liabilities		
Creditors		2490
Expenses Owing		150
		12,770

16.9   Conclusion

Understanding financial statements is an important skill that helps management make different financial decisions for the benefit of the organizations. Unless management are able to grasp what financial statements mean, they cannot escape making wrong decisions that negatively impact their organizations. This chapter has explained cleary what financial statements are and their purposes. The main purposes explained are: determining the financial position of the organization, determining the profitability performance of the organization, and determining the changes in cash flow.

Lucky Yona

Practice Questions

Question 1

(a) What are the problems and limitations related to financial reporting in African countries?
(b) What remedies do you recommend for financial reporting in African business organizations?

Question 2

Explain the significance of financial statements to the following users:

a) Investors
b) Shareholders
c) Lenders
d) Government and their agency
e) Employees
f) Customers
g) Suppliers and other trade creditors

Question 3

AX Company Limited started business on 1st Jan 2020. At the beginning of the year, its financial position as it was reflected in the balance sheet appeared as follows.

AX LTD BALANCE SHEET AS AT 1ST JAN 2020			
	USD		USD
CAPITAL	500,000	FIXED ASSETS	200,000
		CURRENT	
NET PROFIT	100,000	ASSETS	
		BANK	150,000
LONG TERM LIABILITIES	50,000	STOCK	150,000

164

CURRENT LIABILITIES	5,000	DEBTORS	155,000
	655,000		655,000

During the first six months (Jan-June 2010) the following transactions took place:

1. The company paid USD 20,000 (By check) to reduce its long term liabilities
2. The company managed to collect 50% of debts from the trade debtors
3. All current liabilities were paid by check
4. A new Land Cruiser costing USD 15,000 was acquired through a loan from Malawi first bank

REQUIRED

Re-cast the statement of financial position as of 30th June 2010.

Question 4

The following balances were extracted from the books of ABC Ltd as of 31st Dec 2007.

From these balances, prepare the income statement. All Figures are in US Dollars.

Sales ------------------ 16,000,000 Purchases --------- 6,500,000
Returns Inward............ 4,000,000 Returns Outward............ 2,000,000
Salaries and Wages...........1,000,000 Opening Stock------------- 2,500,000
Closing Stock................. 4,600,000 Administrative Expenses 2,000,000
Auditing Fees.................1,000,000 Bad Debts 500,000
Bank Charges----------- 300,000 Loan Interest Expenses 500,000
Debtors .... 400,000 Share Capital 600,000
The country Corporation Tax rate is 30%.

Question 5

A balanced balance sheet reflects the correct financial statements. Discuss.

Question 6

From the following list of balances of Masanja Mkandamizaji Ltd, prepare the comprehensive income statement as well as the statement of financial position as at 30th Dec 2007.

Sales $100,000, Opening Stock $10,000, Purchases $20,000, Wages $15,000, Returns Inward $10,000, Motor Vehicle $100,000, Bank $ 10,000, Debtors $126,000, Creditors $25,000, Loan – National Bank of Commerce $150,000, Owner's Equity $16,000.

Additional Notes

- Depreciation on Fixed Assets is 10%
- Outstanding Wages payable in early Jan 2008 is $ 10,000
- Closing stock is $10,000
- Provision for Bad Debts is 5% of debtors
- The Shareholders withdrawal cash $5,000 from business for personal use.
- The Country corporation tax is only 25%
- During the year goods worth $,1200 were returned to the supplier

Questions 7

Discuss potential issues which are likely to cause untimely financial reports preparation and auditing in your country

Question 8

(a) Discuss the qualitative factors of good financial statements
(b) Explain the factors that can impair the quality aspects of financial statements.

CHAPTER 17

MANAGING THE INTERNAL AUDIT AND EXTERNAL AUDIT FUNCTION

17.1 Introduction

The role of an internal audit in both private and public sector insitutions cannot be over-emphasised as it is clearly known that internal audits help ensure that all internal controls insituted by management to safeguard the organization's assets are working. Managers must understand the role of internal auditors and their own role as managers to avoid unneccesary confusion and misunderstandings between the two parties. Good working relationships between auditors and management need to established and maintained so that audits can conducted effectively. This chapter was written to outline the process of internal auditing, the role of internal auditors, appointment of internal auditors, the role of management in facilitating the internal audit and to touch on external auditing and how management should relate to external auditors.

17.2 Defining Auditing

Auditing is a discipline concerned with the examination of and expression of opinion on the financial statements of an organization. The major concern of auditors is gathering evidence to support or refute information found on financial statements. Auditors aim to prove whether the financial statements gives a true and fair view of the organization's financial standing.

Auditing will, therefore, involve examining completed books of accounts whether prepared manually or electronically, and giving an opinion or a report on the prepared financial statements. It is not the responsibility of the auditors to prepare the financial statements of the organization; this is the responsibility of management of the organization. Managers need to appreciate the different roles of internal and external audits as this appreciation will likely improve corporate governance issues in the organization.

Internal Audits

Internal audits are work of company staff and are not mandatory. In other words, a company may have an internal auditing department or may not. Internal audit function is part of the internal control system of the organization and is more relevant for large organizations with major business transactions or a large number of employees. Small business organizations may not be able to afford to have an internal audit department. The responsibility of establishing internal audits lies in the hands of management as part of their internal control mechanism for safeguarding company assets. In government settings, internal audits are very important but may or may not be required.

External Audits

External auditing is a statutory requirement whereby entities are required to subject their financial statements to auditing by independent firms. The objective of an external audit is to examine financial statements with the aim of being able to give an educated opinion on the accounts and to assess whether they present a true and fair view. The selection of an external auditor is a decision which should be made by the Board of Directors and, in most cases, the shareholders have to assent the appointment done by the board.

17.3   Establishing the internal audit and internal control systems

Management is responsible for establishing the internal audit department. T he internal audit department should be well-staffed with qualified employees able to fulfil the audit function. In many countries, it is mandatory to have an internal audit department in the public sector but optional in the private sector. However, even if your company is a private company, having an internal audit department is very important especially if the company is large and has numerous transactions. Management often make excuses for not employing internal auditors and say that the work can be done by the employed accountants. However, accountants are human beings too and they themselves can commit fraud and override the internal controls causing the organization to lose money or assets. The presence of internal auditors can prevent these actions and protect the company's assets.

When selecting internal audit staff, management should consider qualifications such as CPA (Certified Public Accountant) and CIA (Certified Internal Auditor) for Chief Internal Auditors and senior auditors. Junior auditors should hold Bachelor's degrees in Finance. However, it is also important to consider the competency, experience and background of staff in terms of integrity so as to get the right people in the role of internal auditors.

17.4   The role of internal auditors

Sometimes managers get confused on what internal auditors should be doing and what they should not being doing. It is not the responsibility of the auditors to put in the internal controls systems of the organization into place or to implement the system-- this is purely a management responsibility. Since this is the case, what is the work of an internal auditor?

According to insitute of internal auditors stipulations, the following should be the functions of an internal auditor:

1. Ensure that the internal control systems in place are working efficiently and effectively,

2. Advise management on ways to improve internal control systems, and,

3. Advise management on how to address the weaknesses in the internal control systems.

Internal auditors are the watchdogs of the company . Management should not consider them as intruders or enemies who

17.5   Relating with External Auditors

Chief Executive officers and managers should understand that external auditors are not enemies or witch hunters but they have a role to examine the financial statements and establish whether the financial statements represent a true and fair view of the organizational financial affairs.

Audited financial statements give credibility to the financial statements for external users of the reports such as lenders, investors and the government and its agencies. Where financial statements are not audited by external auditors, they cannot be relied upon .

Chief Executive Officers and managers have a role to support auditors by ensuring that they have access to all required documents to accomplish their assignment.

External auditors are also expected to cooperate with management in the whole process of auditing so as to achieve the proper objectives of the audit.

17.6   Conclusion

Auditing plays a major role in safegauarding companies' asssets and reducing risks. Chief Executive Officers and all management team members should appreciate the role of both internal and external auditors and provide all necessary support to help auditors perform their functions. This chapter intednded to help management to understand what is auditing and differentiate between internal and external auditors. The chapter also explains the role of the internal auditor and how management should set proper internal control systems and how management should relate with the auditors for benefit oif the entire organization.

PractIce Questions

Question 1

Discuss Why Internal auditing is important to an organization

Question 2

What is the role of Management in ensuring that the internal auditing function is working effectively for the benefit of the organization?

Question 3

Discuss how management should relate with both internal auditor and external auditors.

Question 4

Discuss the role of internal auditors and management in setting proper internal controls for the organization

CHAPTER 18

WHISTLE-BLOWING IN AN ORGANIZATION

18.1 Introduction

In the modern world, many organizations are faced with the problem of fraud which leads to cash loss and asset misappropriation. One way of minimizing fraud is for management to set up whistle-blower policies in which employees can safely report fraud and corruption to management. Whistle-blowing means that an employee or group of employees reports another party (be it an employee or third-party) who they suspect is engaging in fraud, misconduct or illegal acts or is failing to act within the prescribed rules and regulations of a specific institution which are likely to have negative impact on the organization.

18.2 The importance of whistle-blowing policies

Management has the responsibility of putting in place a whistle-blower policy that can guide staff and other key stakeholders of the organization on how to report all matters pertaining fraud or other risks to the organization. The whistle-blowing policy provides a formal procedure for handling matters regarding whistle-blowing. It also provides guidelines on how whistle-blowers will be protected and creates openness for those wishing to report a wrong. The policy should encourage employees to air out any concerns or issues affecting the institution freely and without fear.

Whistle-blowing policies:

- Encourage the reporting of corruption and fraud
- Prevent corruption through the deterrent effect
- Gives assurance to whistle-blowers that they will be protected and not subjected to victimization
- Encourage a culture where wrong-doings can be addressed quickly
- Protect a firm in the event of false or malicious accusations through transparency of consequences for these types of claims
- Provide a clear procedure on how to deal with information received from a whistle-blower
- Communicates to staff that their employer takes wrongdoings very seriously and is committed to identifying and remedying them

18.3 The challenges of implementing a whistle-blowing policy

Challenges of implementing a whistle-blowing policy may include the following:

1. **Market-related consequences:** The organization might suffer in case of legal claims or public backlash
2. **Breakdown of trust** between managers and employees
3. **Isolation of whistle-blowers**
4. **Hostility and resentment** from peers and superiors
5. **Broken chain of command** because of fear of going against the company
6. **Poor organisational culture**
7. **Poor infrastructure on reporting** of corruption
8. **Failure to sufficiently protect the whistle-blower**
9. **Lack of support from management**

18.4 Designing a whistle-blowing policy

Like any other policy insituted by an organization, the responsibility of designing and implementing the whistle-blowing policy belongs to management. The board should then approve the policy and ensure that it is implemented by management. In any policy, there are key issues that have to be included in the policy document and for this policy, it must be clear how the whistle-blowing should be handled by both the whistle-blower him or herself and management. The whistle-blowing policy should have the following areas:

c. Background
d. Policy Objectives
e. Scope of the policy
f. Key definitions
g. Reporting by whistle-blower
h. Conducting an investigation
i. Designated Personnel and their roles
j. Protection of the whistle-blower
k. Confidentiality
l. Policy Administration

Sample of Whistle- Blowing Policy #1

1.0. Background

Electronic Inspection Agency was established under the Communications Act no.34 of 2010 of Guandaland. It was charged with the responsibility to inspect all electronic gargets with adherence to international standards on electronic safety. This was necessitated by high number of counterfeit and unsafe electronic equipment in the market. This policy is intended to encourage Board members, staff and stakeholders to report suspected occurrences of illegal, unethical or inappropriate behaviour or practices of corruption and fraud without retribution.

2.0. Scope of the policy

This policy shall apply to the Board, staff and stakeholders of the Agency.

3.0.   Key Definition

In this policy unless the context otherwise requires the words shall have the meaning as provided below:

"**Agency**" refers to Electronic Inspection Agency;

"**Board**" refers to Board of Directors of the Agency;

"**Designated Officer**" refers to staff off the Agency appointed by management for the purpose of receiving the corruption or fraud reports.

"**Whistleblowing**" is the disclosure based on one's reasonable belief that any person has engaged, is engaging or preparing to engage in improper conduct;

"**Whistle blower**" is a person who discloses information of improper conduct in accordance with this Policy;

"**Improper Conduct**" is any conduct which if proved, constitutes a breach of integrity.

4.0.   Reporting by the Whistle Blower

A whistle blower shall make the report in any of the following avenues;

(i)   Toll free telephone number - +00000001

(ii)   Anonymous reporting through the Company's website

(iii) Suggestion boxes in designated areas with no cameras

(iv) Email reporting, Whatsapp, facebook, twiter and other social media platforms.

(v)   Orally to the designated officer or immediate supervisor

5.0.   Conducting investigations

Upon receipt of any report the management shall;

(i)   Verify the authenticity of the report and recommend for further action if necessary and immediate disposal;

(ii)   Classify the report received;

(iii) If significant and needs further assessment, constitute an *ad-hoc* committee to carry out preliminary investigation;

(iv) If the committee is of the view that there is need for specialised investigation, refer the matter for further investigation;

(v) If the committee is of the view that a disciplinary action be taken, refer the matter to HR for necessary action.

6.0. Appointment of the Designated person

The Chief Executive officer of the Agency shall appoint a designated person with the responsibility of receiving any report on corruption and fraud.

7.0. Protection of the Whistleblower

(i) Upon making a disclosure in good faith, based on reasonable grounds and in accordance with and pursuant to this Policy:

    a) Whistleblower shall be protected from any Detrimental Action within the Agency as a direct consequence of the disclosure; and

    b) The Whistleblower's identity and such other Confidential Information of the Whistleblower shall not be disclosed.

    c) The protection against Detrimental Action is extended to any person related to or associated with the Whistleblower.

8.0. Confidentiality

Reasonable steps shall be taken to protect the identity of the whistle blower. The Agency shall engage the National witness protection agency where the matter proceeds or is recommended to legal trial.

9.0.   Policy administration

The Board of Directors shall ultimately be responsible for this policy administration.

The Office of the Chief Executive officer and immediate supervisors as well as the appointed person shall be responsible for the daily implementation of the content of this policy.

This policy shall come into operation upon the approval by the Board.

The management will be responsible to communicate this policy to all employees and where necessary to the Company's stakeholders and the recommend the reviews from time to time.

For enquiry, Please contact:

Designated Person
Corruption prevention Unit
Electronic Inspection Agency

Sample of Whistle-blowing policy #2

Malawi Energy Regulatory Authority (MERA)

1.0   Policy Statement

i. This is policy is designed to enable employees and other stakeholders to air their view concerning the organization on matters accountability and transparency

ii. MERA is committed to promoting the highest level of professionalism, responsiveness, transparency, accountability, ethics and integrity on how it regulates the energy industry.

iii. This Policy is designed to support the MERA's core values in its execution of its mandate

iv. The policy lays down formal procedures for managing disclosing improper conduct that is transparent without compromising the confidentiality of persons involved

2.0.   Definitions

i. **MERA** is the Malawi Energy Regulatory Authority, a corporate body established under the Energy Regulatory Act, 2004.

ii. **CEO** is the Chief Executive Officer of MERA

iii. **Whistleblowing** is the disclosure based on one's reasonable belief that a person has engaged, is engaging or preparing to engage in improper conduct.

iv. **whistle blower** is a person who discloses information of improper conduct in accordance with this Policy.

v. **Improper Conduct** is any conduct which if proved, constitutes a breach of integrity.

vi. **Appointed Officer** is the authorized person appointed to receive reports on Whistleblowing matters.

vii. **Disciplinary Offence** is any action or omission which constitutes a breach as provided by law or the MERA's code of conduct and ethics, policies or a contract of employment.

viii. **Detrimental Action** includes:

    a. Action causing injury, loss or damage;

    b. Intimidation or harassment;

    c. Interference with the lawful employment or livelihood of any person; or

    d. Threat to take any of the actions referred to above.

ix. **Confidential Information**" includes:

    a. Information about the identity, occupation, residential address, work address or whereabouts of:

        i. A whistle blower; and

        ii. A person against whom a Whistle-blower has made a disclosure of improper conduct;

    b. Information disclosed by a Whistle-blower; and

    c. Information that, if disclosed, may cause detriment to any person.

x. **Investigating Officer** means a person assigned to investigate of an Improper Conduct.

Objectives

The objective of this Policy is to:

i. Gives a formal procedure of handling matters regarding whistle blowing

ii. Protect whistle blowers

iii. Create openness for those wishing to report a wrong

iv. Encourage employees to air out any concerns or issues affecting the institution

v. Encourage a culture where wrong doing can be addressed quickly

Scope

This Policy applies to all staff and members of MERA.

Disclosure of Improper Conduct

i.   A staff, member of the board of MERA or third party who becomes aware of an alleged Improper Conduct shall make a disclosure as prescribed in this policy.

ii. For the purpose of this policy an Improper Conduct includes:
   a. Criminal offences, unlawful acts, fraud, corruption, bribery and blackmail;
   b. Failure to comply with legal or regulatory obligations;
   c. Misuse of the MERA's funds or assets;
   d. An act or omission which creates a substantial and specific danger to the lives, health or safety of staff or the public or the environment;
   e. Unsafe work practices;
   f. Abuse of power by an officer of MERA; and
   g. Concealment of any of the above.

iii. The Whistle-blower while making a report needs to have a reasonable belief of the occurrence of Improper Conduct.

iv. In order to give MERA an opportunity to investigate the alleged Improper Conduct and to take the necessary internal corrective actions, Whistle-blowers are encouraged to lodge the following information: -
   a. Description of the people or parties that are involved in the improper conduct;
   b. Details of the Improper Conduct, including the relevant dates of occurrence;
   c. Particulars of witnesses; and,
   d. Particulars or production of documentary evidence.

v.   A disclosure of Improper Conduct may be made even though the person making the disclosure is not able to identify a particular person to which the disclosure relates.

Reporting

i.   A disclosure of Improper Conduct may be made orally in person to the Appointed Officer, via toll free line 0800900600 for both Airtel and TNM networks, in writing via a letter or electronic e-mail to **whistleblow@mera.gov.mw.**

ii. When a disclosure is made orally, the person receiving the disclosure shall produce the same in writing.

iii. If the Improper Conduct involves the Appointed Officer or any of the members of the board of MERA, the Whistle-blower is to report the matter directly to the CEO in case the appointed officer or the Chair of the Board or appointing Authority in case of the members of the Board.

iv. In order to ensure protection of Whistle-blowers, the MERA may outsource the function of reporting of Improper Conduct.

Conduct of Investigation

i.   In respect of disclosures made to the Appointed Officer, he will assess the same to determine whether it is related to an Improper Conduct or excluded from the scope of this Policy. The Appointed Officer shall, within one week from the date the disclosure was made, prepare an assessment report to the CEO appraising him of the result of the assessment, and recommend either to ignore the disclosure or to take further action. The CEO may extend the time for the completion of the assessment report.

ii. In respect of disclosures made against the Appointed Officer or a member of the board, the receiving party shall assess the same to determine whether it is related to an Improper Conduct or excluded from the scope of this Policy before deciding on the next course of action.

iii. For the purpose of the clause above, the receiving party shall be the CEO and the chair of the board or the appointing authority in the case of the Appointed Officer and the member of the board respectively.

iv. Within one week from the date the Assessment Report is received, the CEO or the chair of the board or the appointing Authority as the case may be, shall have the authority to make final decisions including, but not limited to, any of the following:

    a. Rejection of the disclosure(s), either in part or in total, if it falls outside the scope of this Policy;

    b. Directing the matter or any part thereof to be dealt with under other appropriate internal procedures;

    c. Directing an investigation into the disclosure(s) made on any persons involved or implicated;

    d. Designating the Appointed Officer or any other persons from within or outside of MERA to conduct investigations or to take any other action pursuant to this Policy;

    e. Obtaining any other assistance from other parties such as external auditors or obtaining legal advice whether from internal or external advocates; and,

    f. Referring the matter to an appropriate law enforcement agency in case further investigation is necessary.

v. Where the reporting is made to an outsourced function, the assessment report shall be made to the CEO as soon as reasonably practicable.

vi. The Investigating Officer shall have free and unrestricted access to all records of MERA and shall have the authority to examine, obtain or make copies of all or any portion of the contents of documents, files, desks, cabinets, and other storage facilities of MERA so far as it is necessary to assist in the investigation of the Improper Conduct.

vii. At the conclusion of the investigation, the Investigating Officer will submit an Investigation Report of the findings to the CEO, chair of the board, the appointing authority as the case may be.

viii. The Investigation Report will contain the following: -

    a. The specific allegation(s) of Improper Conduct;

    b. All relevant information or evidence received and the grounds for accepting or rejecting them. Copies of interview transcripts and any documents obtained during the course of the investigation shall accompany the investigation report; and

c. The conclusions and recommendations thereof.

ix. The CEO, chair of the board or the appointing Authority shall act in accordance with recommendations of the investigations report.

Confidentiality

Reasonable steps will be taken to maintain the confidentiality of the Whistle-blower's Confidential Information.

Protection of the Whistle-blower

i. Upon making a disclosure in good faith, based on reasonable grounds and in accordance with and pursuant to this Policy:

a. The Whistle-blower shall be protected from any Detrimental Action within MERA as a direct consequence of the disclosure; and

b. The Whistle-blower's identity and such other Confidential Information of the Whistle-blower shall not be disclosed.

ii. The protection against Detrimental Action is extended to any person related to or associated with the Whistle-blower.

iii. A Whistle-blower may lodge a complaint to MERA of any Detrimental Action committed against the Whistle-blower or any person related to or associated with the Whistle-blower, by any employee of MERA.

iv. The Whistle-blower protection conferred under this Policy is not limited or affected notwithstanding that the disclosure of the Improper Conduct does not result in any disciplinary action of the person against whom the disclosure was made.

Administration of the Policy

The Appointed Officer is responsible for the administration, interpretation and application of this Policy.

Roles and Responsibilities

This policy will be implemented by the Director of Human Resource and Administration in collaboration with all Heads of Departments

18.5   Conclusion

The topic of whistleblowing becomes essential to the Chief Executive Officer and managers as it helps them to see organizational risk issues, which through a third party. In this chapter, we discussed the importance of the organization having a whistle-blowing policy and the challenges of implementing a whistle-blowing policy. To help management to design their policies on whistleblowing, a simulated sample of policies from two different organizations is shown in this chapter. The sample policies in this chapter can be used as a model in designing a policy, but CEO's and managers should add or exclude clauses to fit their needs.

Practice Questions

Question 1

Discuss what are likely to be the main challenges of implementing the whistle blowing policies in modern business organization

Question 2

What are the benefits of having a whistle blower policy ?

Questions 3

In designing a whistle-blowing policy, what key issues are important for consideration?

CHAPTER 19

BUSINESS OUTSOURCING

19.1   Introduction

Company CEOs have always faced challenges of cutting costs and maximizing profits for their shareholders. Therefore, being innovative and creative in coming up with different options to help them to achieve the profit-maximization goal requires the use of different strategies. Business outsourcing, apart from cost-saving, is a good strategy that Company CEO'S can use. Business Outsourcing is the process of contracting a portion of a company's activities to third-party providers. Instead of the company doing both core functions and non-core functions, the company might opt to do outsourcing of some of the non- core functions to a third party for a fixed fee.

19.2   Common Reasons for Outsourcing

Companies might opt for outsourcing some of their functions because of several reasons. The reasons will vary from one company to another and there is no legal requirement forcing companies to do so. As CEOs of your company, you require to do a lot of consultation with other members of the management team and come to an agreement to outsource or not to outsource. The following are some of the few reasons as to why a company may seek outsourcing as a business solution :

1. Companies might opt for outsourcing because they want to control expenses.
2. Where it is clear by management with supporting pieces of evidence of financial figures that It is cheap to outsource some services from outside than providing the services internally.
3. Where the company wants to take a competitive advantage by engaging experts in a particular field, that gives an edge compared to other firms in a specific industry.
4. Where the company wants to concentrate on the core business functions instead of engaging in itself on non-core functions.
5. Where the company wants to have better risk management of its businesses.
6. Sometimes outsourcing opted to desire a high level of efficiency and improved quality
7. Sometimes outsourcing is essential to allow Staffing flexibility. Staff relieved of outsourced functions might be allocated to other departments to do different functions

19.3   Factors to consider before outsourcing

A company should consider a number of factors before embarking on outsourcing its functions to another company. These factors should be viewed together rather than in isolation. These are some of the essential elements to consider:

1. If the company has **inadequate skills or capacity to provide a critical service** in the line of the core business, then the need to outsource becomes vital. In this case, consider the size, ability, and availability of the skills in the sought company to provide the service.
2. **Cost of outsourcing or Price of Outsourcing**. When the price of outsourcing is lower than doing the job then outsourcing is much better. However, if it is high and would tie the company's capital in terms of installation and operations, then it would be inappropriate to outsource the function.
3. **Business reputation.** In some cases, outsourcing, if not well managed, could damage or enhance a company's reputation.

Therefore, it is essential to consider possible impacts in this area before outsourcing.

4. **Consider the Risk of what business you are outsourcing.** Some core functions are too risky to outsource.

5. **The Ability to Meet Deadlines.** Consider the ability of the company to meet its obligations on time. There is a possibility of engaging a company which cannot provide the services on time, which at the end may impair the operations of the core functions.

6. **Trustworthiness.** The trustworthiness of the desired company is essential. If we doubt the reliability and integrity of the company, this is too risky to outsource the business functions.

19.4   Benefits of outsourcing

There are several benefits of outsourcing business functions. Some of these benefits we discuss them hereunder :

1. **Get experts in specific areas:** Most of the time, companies do not have all the skills and expertise to do every function that supports business operations. By outsourcing certain services, companies can take advantage of the skills and knowledge that are available in the market.

2. **Reduction of costs:** In some cases, outsourced companies can provide service at lower prices than the primary company itself.

3. **Increased efficiency:** The new service provider might use qualified and experienced staff more efficiently in terms of time and delivery.

4. **Sharing of risks:** In business outsourcing, there is high possibility that your company will be spreading the risk to the other party who has agreed to perform the functions.

19.5   Disadvantages of outsourcing

Despite of the benefits of business outsourcing discussed in the previous section, there are still some disadvantages of outsourcing business functions. The problems mentioned below are not all-inclusive but provide some food for thought for management teams considering outsourcing:

1. **Requires strong communication and collaboration:** To ensure that the organization continues performing well after outsourcing, there is a high need for proper coordination of non-outsourced functions and those not yet outsourced.

2. **Reduces organizational learning by reducing its skill base.** By outsourcing the business functions which staff are not adept in, staff are relieved from some responsibilities and hence they are denied the opportunity to develop their skills in these areas.

3. **Loss of business control:** By outsourcing business functions, there is a high possibility of losing control of the organization as now other company takes over the complete control of the specific service outsourced.

4. **Adverse effect on Morale and Motivation:** It is also possible that employees who are relieved of the functions outsourced might lose confidence and motivation, especially when they are given new responsibilities which may not provide them with the same level of job satisfaction.

5. **Job insecurity:** In some cases, business outsourcing reduces job availability and therefore creates insecurity for current employees.

19.6   Areas of Business outsourcing

There are different areas in which a company can opt to outsource. However, we should note that each organization is different from another. Some are small companies and other larger companies with many departments such that outsourcing might not work for them. One should note that outsourcing core business function might be risk to the organization if the new business provider is not competent and lacks skills and expertise. However, the following are some of functions can be areas where outsourcing becomes vital

1. Knowledge process outsourcing
2. Legal process outsourcing this is for legal advice

3. Research process outsourcing that is for research and analysis function
4. Support service providers
5. Technology / IT Services
6. Marketing
7. Administrative Tasks
8. Bookkeeping / Financial Management

19.7 Conclusion

As business organizations come up with different strategies to improve their efficiency and reduce costs, they may consider business outsourcing as an option to achieve their objectives. This chapter has tried to give an explanation of the concept of business outsourcing by defining the concept and explaining why companies should consider outsourcing.

The chapter has also highlighted the key factors to consider before outsourcing, the benefits of outsourcing, and the disadvantages of outsourcing business functions. Lastly, the chapter briefly highlights the possible areas that companies may consider for business outsourcing. The chapter discussions are not all-inclusive to explain all matters related to business outsourcing. Managers should seek more knowledge about business outsourcing before engaging in it.

Practice Questions

Question 1

Discuss the reasons as to why companies should opt for business outsourcing of its business functions.

Question 2

Discuss the advantages and disadvantages of business outsourcing.

Question 3

What types of business functions can your organization consider them for outsourcing to other companies? Why?

CHAPTER 20

PRIVATE AND PUBLIC PARTNERSHIPS (PPP'S)

20.1 Introduction

Over the years, most countries in the world traditionally financed their investments in infrastructure through reliance of funding through fiscal policies. This means that countries must rely on tax collection from the public to finance infrastructure programs. The private sector has not really been participating in the development of or funding of public infrastructure. However, new trends are emerging from developed countries to involve the private sector in infrastructure work through a model called PPP: Public Private Partnership.

Most countries in the world have adopted PPPs as a strategy to assist governments in financing capital expenditure investments in public sector infrastructure when revenue collected through taxation was insufficient.

The model has now gone global and even developing countries have adopted it. Countries including the Arab Republic of Egypt, Malawi, Mozambique and Tanzania are among the countries that have already established PPPs. There is also a movement in many African countries to create a legal framework to support the use of PPPs in facilitating and managing infrastructure investments.

20.2 What are PPPs?

There are many meanings of the abbreviation of PPP. However, for purposes of this chapter, PPP means "public private partnership". Public private partnerships can be defined as agreements between a government and a private institution under which the government is expected to fund, either partially or in-full, investment in infrastructure development (an asset or social infrastructure) and the private firm delivers the asset or service.

Public private partnership agreements are not limited to physical infrastructure projects but can also include other activities that range from service contracts to concession agreements, privatization or other government supported initiatives.

Donors countries are putting pressure on African governments to legalize public private partnerships in infrastructure development with the notion that the move will increase the private sector's participation in the economic development of the country they exist in.

20.3 Areas for Possible Engagement in Public Private Partnership

There are number of areas where a Public Private Partnership model can work easily. This means that the government can work together in partnership with the private sector in different projects. In all such projects both government and the private sectors agree to provide some funding.

The following are some of the projects where PPP engagements can work

    a. Power generation projects
    b. Water projects
    c. Transportation projects
    d. Other Infrastructure developments

20.4   Key issues to address before embarking on PPP

Any company considering to engage itself with the government on implementing a PPP project should evaluate the costs and benefits of such engagement, otherwise the company mightb suffer in future . PublicPrivate Partnerships Projects are likely to be costly, time consuming, and may pose high risks and negative impact to a company if not carefully selected. Management of the company therefore must do proper evaluation whether the decisions to embark on PPP project is worthwhile to the organization. There should be a win -win situation by both parties. The following key issues have to be evaluated before the organization embarks on PPP's project

a.   The reasons as too why the company wants to embark on the PPP's Project

b.   The cost benefit analyis of the Project to the organization

c.   Availability of resources that we should put in a project

d.   Staffing : Do we have adequate number of staff to engage in the project

e.   Technological capability needed by the project

f.   The existence of robust legal and regulatory framework if it supports the PPP's project

g.   The extent to which stakeholders and beneficiary of the project will be engaged

20.5   Factors for successful implementations of PPPs

Successful implementation of PPP'S Programs requires having in place number of strategies and aplying them from the inception stage of the program to the completion stage of the program. Chief Excutive officers of both private and public sector should work together in ensuring that proper stategies are applied in order to have succefull achievement of objectives of PPP's projects. The following factors are important for consideration of succesfully implementation of the PPP'S.

- **Identification of needs.** Proper identification of the public need that requires the engagement of both private and public institution is important. Not all public need will require the partnership between the public sector and private sector.
- **Creation of a useful regulatory framework**The regulatory framweork is important to enhance easy implemenation of the PPP's . Cumbersome and rigidity in the regulatory and legal framweork can delay implementation.
- **Creation of enabling environment .** The enabling environment such as political environment can enhance easy facilitation in providing the necessary infrastructures needed by PPP's projects.
- **Adequate plans for execution and implementation.** Lack of excution and implemenation plans will delay the completion of the projects
- **Funding plans between the govt and the PPP.** Government willingness to provide fundind as well as the private sector willingness makes easy to implement the projects. Timely release of funding by both parties is also an important factor for the success of the PPP's project.
- **Enforcing contractual agreements**: The contractual agreement between the govt and the PPP must be enforced. There are times when both parties fail to honor the contractual agreement which at the end poses greater risks to projects implementation.
- **Evaluation Mechanisms:** Proper evaluation of project performance periodically is crtical to ensure that they are on course. From time to time it is important to have proper mechanism that helps to monitor the implemenation of the project on day to day basis till the projects are completed on time.
- **Political will and Government Stabililty** : Stability of the government to guarantee confidence in the PPP. Political will of the government to provide continuance support the PPP's is important to ensure succesfully implementation of the project. Political instability of the country impairs the performance of the projects.
- **Governance and Transparency:** There has to be a transparency and good governance environment to ensure that funds are well

utilized, projects are implemented in accordance to envirionmental and technical requirements. Lack of governance can lead to poor quality of the completed projects.

- Institutionalizing anti-corruption polices.
- Provision of Security

20.6   Conclusion

Practice Questions

Questions 1

What are likely to be the impairing factors for implementation of PPP's in most countries?

Question 2

What are key succesfully factors for implemenations of Public Private Partnerships projects?

Question 3

Discuss what factors and issues that have to be considered in the governance and transparency of PPP's.

Question 4

Why should Government embark on PPP'S as option of financing public expenditure on capital goods?

CHAPTER 21

MANAGEMENT OF ORGANIZATION POLITICS

21.1 Introduction

The corporate world is a jungle with its own rules and politics. There is no single organization in the world which lacks elements of politics and yet such politics always have a negative effect on organizational performance. Chief Executives Officers, managers and anybody aspiring to obtain a senior leadership position must understand how to manage office politics in order to progress into a more senior position or to simply maintain the senior position they hold. An inability to effectively handle organizational politics can impair your career progression or lead to the termination of your position as a company CEO or Manager. Some managers try to ignore office politics and pretend as if they don't exist. This way of dealing with office politics can indicate failure of the leader to address concerns and may lead to unresovable conflicts in the future.

It is important for managers to understand the causes of organizational politics in the work place and to know how to manage them in order to retain their own jobs, ensure upward mobility in the company and to minimize the negative impact on operations of these politics.

Organizational politics include all activities performed by individual employees or groups of employees with the intention of tarnishing the image or reputation of their fellow employee(s) for personal interests or gains—usually involving obtaining attention from their superiors. Individuals focused on using organizational politics for self-promtion pay less attention to their work responsibilities, misuse power in order to gain the attention of management and desire to tarnish the images of others in order to elevate themselves .

21.2   Causes of organizational politics

There are many causes of organizational politics in modern organizations. Chief Excecutive Officers and managers need to the key causes and sources of the politics in their organizations so they can effectively manage these situations. Some primary causes of office politics are mentioned below:

- **Lack of trust:** Where there is lack of trust among employees, office politics are likely to develop. Colleagues may not trust each other or there could be distrust between management and their subordinates that goes in both directions.
- **Gossip: This is the result of entertaining rumor information, some people speaking negatives against others to elevate themselves**
- **Feeling of unfair treatment or conditions:** Conflicts due to resource allocation can lead to staff may feeling that the organization treats employees unfairly or unjustly.
- **Nepotism, Tribalism or other Discriminatory practices:** Employees are likely to engage themselves in politics when they find out or suspect that they have missed out on opportunities because of tribalism, nepotism, or for other discriminatory reasons
- **Unregulated conflicting agendas:** When managers are unable to effectively handle individuals and groups with competing and/or personal conflicting agendas, office politics increase
- **Poor relationship** between the CEO, Management, and trade union representatives (OR) between the Chief Executive Officer and the Board of Directors
- **Bullying or disrespect between colleagues** can escalate into work-place conflicts
- **Ignoring irrational or damaging behavior** between colleagues

- **Witch-hunting and gossip** starting from CEOs and Managers or a lack of transparency from these parties
- **Dissatisfaction with renumerations or job responsibilities**
- **Management favoritism** towards certain employees, especially when favoritism is unrelated to good job performance
- **Poor communication** between the CEO and Management team as well as between employees and the management team
- **CEO and/or Management have difficult leadership styles** especially "divide and conquer" leading.

21.3   The Side effects of organizational politics

Organization politics create a number of negative side effects to management, employees and organizations as a whole. First, organization politics can lead to unresovable conflicts between management and employees which,at the end, erode positive relatioships among employees.

Organization politics reduces the productivity of employees, especially the ones who are engaged in it. They will always lack the focus and attention to their activities and will concentrate on idle discussions and waste more productive hours. Their work will always be of substandard performance.

Organization. Politics spoils employees' relationships and workplaces and can create a poor working environment, which can escalate conflicts among employees.

Organization politics tend to demotivate hardworking employees as their contribution and diligence are not noticed or recognized by leaders who entertain politics. This might discourage their commitment to their work. In such a scenario, nonperformer employees have more access to speak to the bosses and get secure promotions and special treatment than the high performers.

In an organization that entertains politics, decision-makers can easily make wrong decisions because they get incorrect information and entertain rumors instead of getting correct information based on facts.

It is also easy to see more stressed employees in an organization where there is too much entertainment of politics by leaders. Divide and rule principle is more applicable in such an environment as the bosses will have a group of those he/she dislikes and those who are more likely.

Organization politics does not provide transparency of information between management and employees. Employees might always not knowing what is happening at the organization, but here rumors from the streets.

21.4   Strategies to manage organizational politics

As a CEO of your organization, remember that each organization has its own policies and so you will need to devise and implement strategies that will help you sustain your position. Managing organizational politics is situational--meaning that you will have to use a combination of different strategies to address the various causes of these politics. Strategies which have worked to solve the issue of organizational politics in one place may fail in your organization. However, having a list of strategies to work from can help you get a start on reducing politics in the work place. Here are some suggestions:

a.   Create a work environment that is conducive and motivating
b.   Be transparent
c.   Promote teamwork
d.   Improve communication channels
e.   Try to stay impartial
f.   Interact regularly with employees in a positive way
g.   Conduct meaningful team-building activities
h.   Create and utilize grievance procedures and responses

21.5   Conclusion

Organization politics is a broader topic that might require more scholarly discussion and more reading of different researched papers. However, this brief topic on the subject has tried to underscore some relevant critical issues related to organizational politics which can help the Chief Excutive Officer and managers to cope with such politics.

The issues discussed could help Chief executive officers and managers with no background on the subject matter can to quickly grasp the concepts and apply them in their work environment.

The key issues discussed in this chapter include the definition of organization politics, causes of organization politics, the Side effects of organizational politics, and strategies that management can use to manage corporate politics.

Practice Questions

Question 1

What are the common causes of organizational politics?

Question 2

Discuss the strategies which the CEO and Managers can use to mitigate organizational politics

Question 3

Discuss the consequences of poor management of organizational politics at company level

Question 4

Discuss the consequences of relying on wrong information through rumors in decision making for the Chief Excutive Officer and other managers.

Question 5

Organization politics cannot be eliminated in all companies and organizations. In other words they are there to stay . Discuss.

ALSO, BY LUCKY YONA

This book is intended to be used as a textbook in Financial Accounting for Executive MBAs candidates. This book has simplified the subject matter and gives understanding that can be easily applied by Executives as they try to manage their organizations. The author believes that this book will meet the needs of Executives who study Financial Accounting as a module in their course. The book is presented in a simple language which will make the subject not only interesting but also enjoyable for the learners.

This book is intended to be a textbook in International Finance. As a textbook, it covers most of the theories and concepts in the field, clearly explaining concepts and theories with practical application to developing countries environment and can help students to understand how international finance concepts are applicable in the business world. The author believes that this book will meet the needs of students undertaking MBA courses in International Business and Trade and other professional courses such as CPA, CIMA CFA and ACCA.The presentation of this book is in a simple language, which makes the reading interesting and enjoyable to both students and managers in this field.

This book is intended to bridge a gap on non-availability of Corporate Finance textbooks. In order to respond to this need, the book has been developed to provide reading materials in various topics on Corporate Finance. The book is intended to be used as a textbook as most of the theories and concepts in the field are clearly explained with practical mathematical calculations that clearly help to understand how the concepts are applicable in the business world. The author believes that this book will meet the needs of students undertaking MBA courses and other professional courses in CPA, CMA CFA and ACCA. The book is presented in simple methodology which will make Corporate Finance interesting, enjoyable and will provide both students and managers in the field with understanding of the subject matter.

This book is all about public finance and contemporary issues in taxation. The book discusses about contemporary issues in taxation that cater across all developing countries as well as discusses the concept of public debts and balance of payments. These are related issues that are critical for the economic development of a country. Students undertaking their undergraduate studies, postgraduate studies, and professional studies will find the book to be useful and full of knowledge in the various issues that affect taxation in their countries.

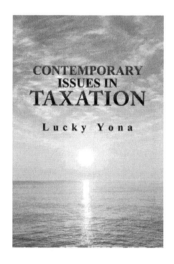

The dominant capital structure studies across the globe have been concentrated in developed countries and specifically for listed companies and few on unlisted companies or mixed companies. This thesis aims to examine the extent to which company liquidity, profitability, tangibility, and company size influence the leverage of Tanzanian companies as suggested by pecking order and trade-off theory. The study findings show a negative relationship between company liquidity and company leverage as measured by debt ratio and debt-to-equity ratio. These findings show the validity of the pecking order theory in Tanzania. The postulates of the trade-off theory as far as liquidity is concerned are not valid. The study findings also reveal a positive relationship between profitability and leverage, suggesting that majority of Tanzanian companies used more debts as the means of financing their business operations despite their profitability. The study also found that the tangibility of listed companies was higher than that of the unlisted companies and that there was a negative relationship between tangibility and leverage, which is valid to pecking order but contrary to trade-off theory. As far as company size is concerned, study findings suggest that pecking order theory (POT) and trade-off theory (TOT) relevance cannot be fully supported in Tanzanian companies as the findings have revealed a negative relationship between company size and leverage. Findings reveal a negative relationship between company size and leverage. Pecking order theory (POT) and trade-off theory (TOT) relevance cannot be fully supported in Tanzanian companies, and size of listed companies was higher than that of the unlisted companies. This suggests that the size of majority of Tanzanian unlisted companies is still small as compared to the listed companies

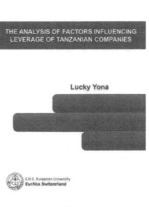

THE ANALYSIS OF FACTORS INFLUENCING LEVERAGE OF TANZANIAN COMPANIES

Lucky Yona

E.H.E. European University
EurAka Switzerland

Printed in Great Britain
by Amazon

87275946R00135